PLEASE, GOD, I'M A CITY GIRL. WHAT AM I DOING IN THE COUNTRY?

Adventures With God

By

Lola M. Autry

Other books by the author

FIFTY-TWO DEVOTIONAL PROGRAMS for PRIMARY
CHILDREN, With Original Songs.
   Published by Baker Book House

BIBLE PUPPET PLAYS
   Co-authored with Ewart A. Autry
   Published by Baker Book House

DON'T LOOK BACK MAMA
   Co-authored with Ewart A. Autry.
   Hardcover A Maverick Publication
   Soft cover published by Whippoorwill Valley
   Publishers

THE TURTLE and the OAK
   Co-authored with Ewart A. Autry
   Soft Cover. Published by Whippoorwill Valley
   Publishers

DEDICATION

This book is dedicated to our LORD and Saviour,
Jesus Christ

It is the author's hope that He will be glorified through
these words and that all who read them will be led to follow
Him wherever He leads.

CONTENTS

PREFACE

This story is about God and me, but it is also about you and God. He will carry you through many experiences and adventures, both good and bad, if you commit to His leadership. The difference in God's experiences and adventures to our man made ones lies in Who He is. His purposes are not always ours. His thoughts are higher than our thoughts, and His ways are more deliberate. He knows what He is doing, where He is leading, and the end results. These differences make following Him worthwhile even though they sometimes lead to things we would rather not have to face.

The Apostle Paul was "sold out to Christ." He suffered pain, sorrow, heartache, beatings, stonings, shipwrecks. Yet he counted it all worthwhile when he remembered what Jesus did that he (Paul) might be saved.

My life has been a relatively happy one. I have suffered, but not to the extent Paul did. There have been sorrows, heartaches, poverty, illnesses and deaths. But the joy of His love, compassion, fellowship, leadership, and salvation have made me a very blessed, happy and contented Child of God. I thoughtfully, prayerfully, and whole-heartedly recommend Him to you.

I pray that reading bits of my "journey" will cause you to want to walk with Him daily.

Lola M. Autry

PART ONE

THE DECISION

When FAITH walks by and takes your hand you are often led to strange places and great adventures. That is why I found myself on a hillside deep in a heavily wooded land. My preacher husband and I had followed FAITH from the city to the place of his birth that we might serve country churches. There were many questions for me. I had never lived in the country. I was accustomed to conveniences—electricity, city water, telephones, paved streets, next door neighbors, sidewalks, concerts, operas, intellectual lectures, doctors and hospitals close by. There would be none of those in the area where we would be.

"Maybe we can visit the city occasionally," my husband consoled. That, I knew, would not be likely in this barely-at-the-end-of-the-Great-Depression era. Country churches did not have large budgets. Most had no budget. The preacher's salary would be more like chickens and eggs, an occasional sack of home made sausage, dried ears of corn for milling into meal to make cornbread, and in the fall of the year—sweet potatoes. This would all be good and appreciated, but there had to be some money to buy gas and tires for a car, and coffee, flour and sugar. Money would be extremely scarce. "Sometimes," Ewart told me, "we might receive fresh sorghum molasses as part of the salary. You'll like that!"

I wasn't so sure about sorghum molasses. All I knew in the molasses area was Log Cabin Maple Syrup that was sold in a little tin can in the shape of a log cabin. The chimney of the cabin served as the pouring spout. That was about my nearest acquaintance to country living.

Music had always been a major love of my life, and I had had a choice of attending medical school or being a concert pianist. Since the time I was twelve years old I had almost daily singing or piano playing programs for local radio stations. I enjoyed that. My college degree was in music and science. What good would that do me where we would be living?

FAITH kept trying to assure me that all would work out to God's glory if I would commit to being guided by the Holy Spirit. The time finally arrived when we prayed,

"Lord, even if we have to sleep on the ground because we have no other place, just assure us of an oak tree under which to lay a pallet and a stone for a pillow."

FAITH took our hands and our hearts, and we moved to the country. Adventure, coupled with learning, was to become my daily feast.

PART TWO

THE STRUGGLE

WHEN IGNORANCE AND BLISS MEET THEY DO NOT BOW POLITELY

City Sidewalks and Hip Boots

I looked at the pair of sleek high-heeled shoes I held in my hand. I had shopped for them until the exact right pair had been brought to me. Shoes were a weakness. To me they were symbols of grace and chic and status, and I loved them. Then I looked at my feet. There was no beauty, no grace and no status to the black, hip-high rubber boots I had on, and the mud and slush of the swamp that lay ahead was not even a distant cousin to the smooth sidewalks of the city. I didn't know what a swamp was, but I was told to put on boots, so I did. It's not that I was all that obedient to commands. The fact was, *I was ignorant*. And I was about to learn just how much I did NOT know.

My preacher husband, Ewart, and I had moved from the city to serve country churches. This was no church to which I was on my way. It was an unknown destination—a swamp. Whatever that was! A turtle, rare and ugly, yet exotic to my untrained eye, slid off a log resting on the murky water. It later came up from its dive, stuck its head above the water, looked at me and went under again. Perhaps we both judged each other as ugly. I certainly felt that way.

We had to wade across this swamp to reach the favored fishing place my husband had chosen. We sat there all day holding a cane pole with a stout cord attached to it, and to the cord a fishhook baited with icky, slimy worms inched onto it. Nothing happened. The things we caught were limbs hiding below the surface of the water and a sunburn from the summer sun.

Trudging back through the stagnant water of the swamp I grumbled to myself, "What am I doing in the country?" If this day was a sample of that well-touted country bliss, I wondered what would be in store for the time to come. But, I wanted to be a good sport—to do whatever would make my husband happy, and I had never seen him more relaxed and cheerful than now.

It was not until many years later, when we gave each other brand new pairs of rubber hip boots as Christmas gifts, that he learned how much I feared that swamp, yet how much I trusted his woodland knowledge and his ability to protect me.

This day all I wished for was the ease of walking on a city sidewalk in a pair of beautiful shoes.

Turnip Greens and Hog Shorts

Spring had come after a cold, cold winter. The creek below our house had been free of ice for a couple of weeks. The earth was warming, and we planned to have a garden. I had never gardened, nor had I cooked very much. My mother-in-law, bless her heart, taught me how to make biscuits, but I never could prepare vegetables the way she did. Mine always tasted "citified". Hers were wonderfully country. I was determined to learn her way of cooking turnip greens, so we sowed those seeds early. The little darlings came up. <u>Every one of them.</u> Ewart explained that was the way it should be. As the leaves grew and crowded each other the plants would be thinned by pulling them up and using them. That would allow those left to grow larger.

Early one morning I went to the garden and gathered what I thought would be enough of the greens for our meal. I washed them in the creek water. It was clear and pure. Proudly, I put them on to cook, picturing in my mind how the dish would look, prematurely tasting them even before they had begun to boil. Mealtime came and I displayed my culinary art.

My husband took one look at them, folded me in his arms, and said, "Honey, you're supposed to discard the roots before you cook the leaves, but because these greens and roots are so young and tender we're going to eat them all." And we did. Eventually, I learned to cook greens the way his mother did—without the roots.

The number of times I asked myself what I was doing in the country was growing, but the top number had not yet been reached. I was not unhappy about where we lived, I simply felt so inadequate. A few days after the turnip green episode my brother-in-law came over to visit a few minutes. He and my husband were two of five living children in the family. They had been reared on the land where we now lived. In fact, our house was the one in which my husband and his brother had been born.

As they did their brotherly talking, my brother-in-law said, "I plan to put soda around the corn in the fields today." Not even thinking that I was intruding on their conversation I asked, "How can you put soda around each of those corn stalks in those huge fields in one day?" You see the only soda I had ever heard of was Arm and Hammer Baking Soda that came in those little orange boxes. I envisioned many, many little boxes, and him kneeling and sprinkling a tablespoon or so of that kind of soda around each stalk. Well, between hearty laughs he and my husband explained, "It's not baking soda. This is Sodium Nitrate, a fertilizer." My courses in chemistry had not helped one bit. I could understand how ridiculous my ignorance made me appear, and I joined in the laughter, but that did not take away the sting of being ignorant.

The question about the soda, however, could never compare with another a few days later. Ewart and I were going to our little country town and his brother said to him, "Will you get my hogs some shorts?" At least I had presence of mind enough not to blurt out the question that came to mind. When my brother-in-law had gone I smiled at my husband and asked, "Why do hogs need shorts?"

He tried to keep from laughing, but a giggle had to burst out. Again he took me in his arms. He always did that when he was trying to explain things that puzzled me about the country. "Princess," he said. He often called me Princess because I told him one time that I felt like a fairy princess lost in the woods. "Hogs don't *wear* shorts. They *eat* them."

I was more confused than ever. Why would hogs eat shorts? Then he explained, "The hog feed kind of shorts are not made of cloth. They are the husks from grains, and they are very good for them."

The Other Side of Ignorance

Our church people were afraid of me!

In my wildest dreams I had never thought of being feared, but I was. I don't know why country people of that day thought city folk were smarter than they, but they did. In one sense they looked *up* to me as a superior. In reality, I looked *down* on me as an almost total ignoramus. The truth was we were simply ignorant of each other's ways.

The most fear seemed apparent in my new neighbors.

The first time I entered the church that would eventually become my home church, there was a sudden hush. A curiosity about me was evidenced in an evasive eyeing from the women and an almost palpable sense of fear that this woman from the city would not accept them. A small bit of defiance was also present—a sense of withdrawal that proclaimed, "If she's snooty, we can be, too." They couldn't see the racing of my heart, the trembling of my knees and the need for their acceptance of me.

One of the first things to be learned was that many country communities were, and some still are, clannish. There is a stand-off-and-observe period before an "outsider" is considered one of the clan. Initially, there is an outgoing welcome to visitors, but when the first meeting is past, the time has come for that visitor to prove he or she is worthy of acceptance. My husband had grown up in this area. He was known and loved, but at this point I was beyond the visitor status and in the "wait and see" mode.

In the city I sometimes did not know the names of my near neighbors. In the country area where our home was there was a saying, "If you move to our community you'd better not say anything bad about a person because everybody's kin to everyone else." That's not a bad way to keep down gossip.

Never had I been in this type situation. In the city there was no such strong sense of family and community. I felt secure because my husband was seemingly kin to everyone. I was determined to pass the community scrutiny. I wanted to be accepted and loved. And I tried. Relatives might be as distant as fifth or sixth cousins but the kinship was known. Everyone, even those fifths or sixths, were called "Cud'n", and were vital parts of the greater family. I soon became known as Cud'n Lola Mae to a host of people.

I knew I had passed the test when we were having a meal with a family who were members of one of the churches.

During our lunch I called the mother of our host by her married name. She stopped eating, held her knife in one hand and her fork in the other and said, firmly but lovingly, "Honey, my name is not Mrs. to you. It is Cud'n…!" We were no longer fearful of each other. We had learned that to be educated meant more than where you lived and what educational degrees you could add to your name. The greatest education came with love and understanding.

Why Didn't He Stay in One Place?

To be truly at home in the country became my goal. One of the things that troubled me most was that I was afraid of my surroundings. In the city there were street names and signs giving directions. In our wooded area I found none of those. To be out of sight of the house was to be lost. My woods-wise husband was never lost.

Once we had gone walking. He told me to wait where we were. His keen eyes had spotted something he wanted to investigate a few yards away. I waited. Finally he called. "Come over here, Honey. I want to show you something."

We were in a little creek valley surrounded by high hills. I started to him in the direction of his voice. The next time I heard him call he seemed farther away. The third time, I could barely hear him. "He's moving," I said aloud. "I'll never find him." I tried calling out to him. Faintly, I heard him say, "Stand still. I'm coming to you."

He was smiling when he came into sight—just a little bit. I had no clue as to why he was smiling until he said, "You were falling for one of Nature's tricks. I should have warned you about it. In a valley like this one surrounded by hills, sounds bounce off as echoes and seem to come from different directions. You were walking away from me rather than toward me because you followed the wrong signal."

How like so many of us, I thought. God sends out His

call and we want to follow His directions but we lose our bearings because of all the mixed signals we get.

Fear Can Be a Booger

Early one morning several days later he said, "Honey, I've got to finish this magazine article I'm writing. Our fishhooks at the creek need to be checked to see if we've caught anything. Do you think you could do that while I finish this?"

"I don't know," I stammered. "I've never been to the creek by myself."

"You'll make it fine," he said. "I blazed you a tree trail yesterday." For you who are not knowledgeable of country ways, blazing a tree trail means making a mark on a tree by chipping out a small piece of the bark. One tree leads to another until the destination has been reached.

Autry Creek was about three hundred yards from the house, but when enveloped in a maze of trees, none of which you recognize—they're all just trees. I was scared of the woods, but with false bravado I started toward the creek. As soon as I found the first tree blaze I looked back toward the house. I could still see it, so I ventured to the next tree. There was the mark. I followed each one until finally I heard the gentle calling of the creek water. I ran toward it as fast as I could. When I reached the creek bank I breathed a fervent, "Thank You, Lord." I gave Him all the praise. After all, it had to be He who inspired my husband to mark that trail.

We had put out several baited hooks the evening before. From where I stood I could count six bobbing poles. That meant we had caught something. All went well as I pulled out the first five with their catch. We would have fish for our noon meal. The sixth was a different matter. Whatever was on it had pulled the pole deep into the water. Apparently the hook had become entangled on tree roots that extended into the water from the bank.

What would Ewart do about this? I thought. I knew the answer. I had seen him solve this problem before. Following his example, I stepped cautiously into the waist-deep water, grasped the end of the submerged pole and pulled gently. That's when the creek waters exploded. The pole and its hook and line had been released from their prison. All around me the thing hanging from the end of the line, held firmly by the hook, was what I thought was the meanest looking, largest, most horrible snake ever imagined. I threw the pole and its catch as far onto the creek bank as I could, climbed out of the water and ran.

I was screaming for my husband as I neared the house. "Help!" I shouted. "There's a snake!"

Ewart hurried toward me. "Where is it?" he asked calmly, and I wanted to choke him. There was a snake at the creek and my husband was as unexcited as if it had been a daffodil.

"On one of the fish hooks at the creek," I said.

We walked to the place where I had flung the pole onto the bank. The pole wasn't there. It was back in the creek, moving slowly upstream. "He must have wiggled himself and the pole back into the water," Ewart explained.

"I don't ever want to fish here again," I murmured angrily. "I never ever saw a snake in the city." Then I bit my lip for having said that. I knew it wasn't so. I had seen one when I was a little girl. It was in one of my mother's flowerbeds. She didn't make a great to-do over it. Why should I?

I squared my shoulders, took a deep breath and followed my husband in the direction the pole was moving. It stopped at a small drift in the creek.

Ewart—brave man, I thought—took off his shoes and stepped into the cold creek water. "What are you doing?" I asked anxiously. I was shocked that he was going after that pole and the long thing at the end of the line. "I'm going to see what kind of snake it is," he said. "Want to join me?"

"No way," I told him.

The crystal clear water was not quite as deep here as it had been where the hooks were. He peeped cautiously to see if he could spot what was on the hook that was again hung on tree roots. Before I could beg him not to do so, he bent over, put his hands on the line and followed it to the hook. I stood, sobbing.

I heard him laugh. "Have you lost your mind?" I stammered. "What are you doing?"

He grabbed the end of the pole and began to wade toward the bank, still chuckling. I screamed when he placed the catch down, a good distance from me, "Be careful!"

He smiled at me with that amused "you poor little ignorant city girl" look. "Princess," he said, "it can't hurt you. This isn't a snake. It's a fresh water eel. Some people like to eat them."

Scaredy-cats Often Have Great Imaginations

One morning, after an early breakfast, we decided to go for a walk in the woods. We followed the bends of the creek until we came to a large tree. I had no idea what kind it was. My husband said, "You sit here and rest against this tree. I'm going to walk a little farther. I'll be back soon."

The sun was trying to peep through the denseness of the woods and mirror itself in the creek waters. The reflection was so beautiful that I looked in the creek at myself. I didn't see much of beauty. You certainly do not look as you did in the city, I thought. You have on no makeup. Even though your hair is combed it is certainly not very stylish, and your clothes definitely would not be worn in the city. I walked back and sat beneath my tree.

Ewart's "be back soon" turned into a long while as far as I was concerned. The peace and quietness around me had been soothing and relaxing, and I knew I was falling in love with this place where God had stationed me. But now, instead of concentrating on that, I began to imagine what would happen if Ewart had an accident and could not get to me. I had no clue as to where he was. I had no idea how to get to the house. I could follow the creek back, but I didn't know where to leave it and turn toward home. I called to him. There was no answer.

A squirrel barked at me from the top of the tree where I sat. A blue jay spotted me and warned all other creatures nearby of a stranger in the midst. The wind in the trees began to whisper. "Stop making fun of me," I whimpered. "I know I'm a stranger, but I'm really trying to make a good home here. I believe I could truly love this place if I were not so afraid."

About that time I heard a crashing sound about a hundred yards from me. I looked in the direction of the crashing, but couldn't see through the underbrush. I was terrified, shaking, holding my breath in fear. My imagination went rampant. *What if that's a bear? Or a coyote? Or a cougar? Or a wolf? Or even a wild dog? They run in packs. What will I do?* I pushed myself into as small an object as I could against the tree where I sat. I heard the crashing noise again. It was nearer. It was loud.

By this time I was hysterical. I screamed. Whatever was coming began to run. Above the approaching noise I heard my husband's voice. "I'm coming! I'm coming!" he shouted. He was carrying an enormous gathering of leaves in his arms. He hurled them to the ground and reached for me. "What's the matter?" he gasped. "What's wrong?"

"Nothing now," I sobbed. When you were gone so long I thought some wild animal had attacked you or you had been hurt some other way and would never be able to come back. I didn't know what to do." He just held me tightly and stroked my hair. "My imagination did it to me again," I confessed.

He loosed his grip on me slowly and looked into my face. "Did you see all those leaves I was carrying?" he gently asked. I nodded. "They were to be a part of your country education, to give confidence in this land where we serve God Who created it. Let's pick them up, and as we look at them you'll understand."

This was a *big* pile of leaves and twigs. The crashing noise I had heard was he coming through the underbrush. He was a tall man, a great woodsman. He could move as quietly as a worm across the forest floor when it was necessary, but when he was not trying to do that he could make a lot of noise.

For two hours we sat and studied leaves. I became adept at telling which leaf belonged to a particular specie of tree. Those were the moments when my love and friendship for trees began. They were to become my street signs, my woodland guide posts, my helpers.

Country ways were becoming an ever-educating part of my life, and I loved the learning. My imagination was still alive, but I began to realize neither the people nor the land was a threat.

ENTERTAINING JUST "AIN'T" THE SAME

*The Watermelons Are Ripe and There's Singing
To Be Done.*

M y adventures with God were ever varied, and each was enlightening. In the city entertaining was formal to an extent. I tried that approach in the country. It was not the same. There is camaraderie in the country that is built on family, friendship and hospitality. They work together to provide a joyful, relaxed time. Often on Sunday afternoons or during Revival Service times the young people of a church would band together and go to one house for an afternoon of fun and companionship. They would gather around a piano, if there was one in the home, and sing for an hour or more. They might go to the swimming hole in the river or creek and then visit, unannounced, someone's watermelon patch. This was an expected prank that no one thought anything about. Patch owners played a game familiar to both sides. Often an owner would hide in his patch when he knew kids were going to visit it. If he spotted them he jumped and scared them. When they ran, he called them back and told them, "Make yourselves at home." Parents just laughed and older adults grinned. Young children looked forward to having a juicy melon.

Many times the preacher and his family looked forward to melon-eating time, too. The actual eating was usually done outside and the meat of the melon bitten from the rind. There were no "clean-ups" that way, except to discard the rind properly.

We Like Our Guests to Make Themselves at Home

One time Ewart, the children and I were invited to the home of some church members for the evening meal. The house was very small and run-down. The host family was looking forward to the next year when they could build a new house. Meanwhile they were doing what all country people of the near-post-depression days were doing— making out with what they had. We thought nothing of it. Our circumstances were barely better than theirs.

We would be eating in the kitchen. The house was too small for a separate dining area. The kitchen floor slanted downhill. Straight back, cane-bottomed chairs had been placed at the table. The preacher's chair was always at the head. Ewart sat down and leaned back. The chair leaned back, too. It had been used as a makeshift rocker for lulling babies to sleep, and the rear legs were worn into the same slant as that of the floor. Chair and preacher both landed on their backs on the floor.

My astonished husband was in a seated, lying-down position. About that time the man of the house walked in and assessed the situation. From his lofty six-foot-three height he grinned and held out his hand of welcome and said, "Well, Preacher, we always do like for our guests to make themselves at home." The feast his wife had prepared went off beautifully. A relaxed, fun-filled evening ended all too soon. There was no embarrassment. There was no need for any.

Country people were full of humor and understanding.

He Took Off His Shoes. "Where Am I Sleeping?"

A pastor-friend from nearby dropped in one night. He had come to meet the city pastor who was preaching the Revival Meeting services at our church that week. We thought he would stay an hour or so and go home, but near bedtime we noticed he was sitting around in his sock feet. Soon he asked, "Where do you want me to sleep?" We had no spare bedroom. We had given our bedroom to our friend from the city, and we were bedding down on pallets in the children's room.

"What are we going to do?" I whispered to Ewart. "I can make him a pallet, but the only large space we have for him to sleep is in the kitchen under the table."

Now my husband knew a lot more about country ways than I. He said to me, "Make it there. It'll be all right."

Embarrassed almost to the point of tears, I showed him his "bedroom". "I'm so sorry we have no other place for you," I apologized.

"Don't worry about it," he said. "You just haven't been out here long enough to know that if you are a preacher, anything can happen to you. I'll sleep real good right here, and don't let this bother you at all. I'll just make myself at home."

The Chicken That Was

One Sunday in the late '40's we were to have dinner with one of the church deacons and his wife. It might be well to explain here that in that era dinner was at noon, supper about six o'clock. There was no time called lunch. The middle of the day spread was always a large one. Also, the custom was for the pastor and his family to have meals on Sundays with church families.

I had heard my mother-in-law, also a preacher's wife, tell of the custom in her day. There was only one church meeting each month, and to prolong the fellowship after worship the entire congregation went home with the preacher and his family. One time she cooked three hams, with all the "fixin's" including vegetables, homemade biscuits and cornbread. "Thank you, Lord, that it's not that way anymore," I muttered in a whisper. "I don't think I could handle it." There came a gentle nudge to my brain that said, "You could if I asked you and you were willing to follow Me." I hung my head and a tear ran down my cheek. "Forgive me, Father," I prayed silently, "for forgetting that You enable us to do whatever You lead us to do."

On this Sunday, so long ago, when we were to go to the deacon's house, a strange thing happened. He was not present for Sunday School or for the Worship Service. His wife was. My preacher husband, in a gentle teasing way, said to her, "Where's your husband today? Did he stay at home to fix dinner for us?"

She giggled. "No. He'll tell you about it when you see him."

Their house was very near the church and we walked with his wife to it. Our deacon friend met us at the door. "Come in," he invited, and held the door for us to enter. I followed his wife to the kitchen, as was the custom, to put the already prepared food on the table. He and Ewart stood in the dining area and talked.

Soon our hostess showed us where we were to be seated. The deacon did not sit. He stood at a nearby sideboard.

"Aren't you joining us?" my husband asked.

"Not today, Preacher," he said. "I'll just stand here and eat, but you sit down. We want our guests to make themselves at home."

"Then, if you really mean you want me to make myself

at home, I'll join you," Ewart said. He picked up his plate and eating utensils and moved to stand beside our host.

"I guess I'd better tell you why I'm standing up to eat and why I wasn't at church," confessed our friend. He turned his eyes, pleading for understanding, first to my husband, then to me. "It was like this," he began. "Early this morning my wife asked me to kill a rooster for dinner today. I kept putting it off. She kept reminding me. Her reminding turned into what I considered nagging." He looked at her apologetically. "I'm sorry, Honey," he said, "but that's the way it seemed to me." He picked up the story. "Finally I grabbed my old single shot, 30 inch barrel, 12 gauge shotgun and went to the kitchen window.

"The chickens were feeding right in front of it. I opened the window, took aim and fired. I sent that rooster to kingdom-come." He paused, looked at us, and continued. "Preacher," he blurted, "the reason I'm not sitting down to eat is that I was so mad because my wife kept telling me what to do that I wasn't listening. I didn't hear her when she said, 'This wood cook stove is too hot. I'd better open the oven door and let some heat out so my biscuits won't burn.'

"And—as you know—that wood cook stove is just about three feet away from that kitchen window, and the oven door opens toward it. When I pulled the trigger of that old gun, that 'blasted' (forgive me, Preacher, for that word) gun kicked me so hard that I sat down on that hot oven door. That's why I'm not sitting at the table. It would be too painful."

"Are we having rooster for dinner today?" my husband teased.

"Nope. There was nothing left of him but feathers."

Moral of this story: a hot temper combined with a hot oven door puts one in a hot predicament.

A Man's Tears

Men usually do not shed tears as easily as women. This seems to be true regardless of the place. I only saw my father cry one time in my life. That was when my mother was dying. We lived in the city. He was the only man I had even seen cry. So, I especially did not expect to see a brawny, country man crying as he stood at our front door one night. Between sobs he said to my husband, "Can you and the missus and kids come and stay at my house as long as I need you? I'd want you to make yourselves at home. It won't be like I'd be entertaining you, but I do like for folks to feel at home."

"What's the problem?" my puzzled husband asked. "Why is it so important that we move into your house?"

"I just took my wife to the hospital," he said, "and the news is not good. My wife is worried about our children. There's no one to take care of them except me, and the doctor said I need to be with her. That's where I want to be, Preacher, but somebody's got to help me. Will you?"

"Let me get my family together," he said, "and we'll be right over. Try to wait for us long enough to show us where things are."

We knew there were three small boys in that home ranging in ages 4 to 7. They were good kids. We'd have no problems that way. What we didn't know were other conditions. Was there food in the house? Where would we sleep? Would all of us be in one room? We didn't even know the layout of the house. This was winter, and at night. There was snow on the ground with ice as its foundation. Would there be stacked wood on the porch with which to feed the open fireplace that was standard heating?

As I gathered clothes and milk and bottles and other necessities for our children and us, I thought of the city, and warmth and convenience and paved streets cleared of snow and ice. There was none of that here. There was, however, an abundance of one thing that knows no territorial boundary—love. That love would have to suffice regardless of circumstances.

It is not difficult to love little children. Those at the house were quiet, teary-eyed. They knew their mother was sick and their daddy was going to be with her. The boys knew us from Sunday School, but they were still somewhat skeptical of our presence. We talked to them softly and gave each a hug as we explained the plan: we would stay with them for as long as their mom and dad were away.

The children had not had supper. Neither had we. The only food I could find to prepare consisted of the ingredients to make some biscuits and gravy, using the lard rendered from frying fatback hog meat (sometimes called salt pork). This type gravy was known in the area as sawmill gravy because that was the usual breakfast food, sometimes with eggs, eaten by men who ran the sawmills that were dotted across the woodlands. Add a little sorghum molasses and home-churned butter, and the meal was called good.

Bedtime came early and as I rummaged around looking for sheets and quilts to keep us warm through the night I realized there need not have been an invitation for us to make ourselves at home. We had to do that by necessity. The suddenness with which the woman had become ill had left no time for preparation for others to be in the house.

The three boys slept together in one bed on one side of the fireplace room. The parents' bed was on the other side. There was no guest bedroom, and no other beds. We had three children of our own with us. My husband, our oldest little boy and I could sleep in the only available bed, but our twins were just six months old. I could not visualize the five of us in one bed. For fear of rolling over on one of the babies, if we tried that, I would sit up in a chair and get what sleep I could. That wouldn't work either. My husband would sit up with me. He was fearful of rolling over on one of the children, too. We looked around for something to use as a makeshift bed for our wee ones.

Ewart went to the kitchen. I heard him say, "Aha!"

"What was that 'aha' all about?" I called.

"I've found a bed for the twins," he answered.

"In the kitchen?"

"Yep. I'm on my way with part of it."

He entered carrying two kitchen chairs which he placed seat to seat, then pushed their sides against the bed. Back he went into the kitchen and brought out two more chairs. He placed them next to the first two. The backs of the four chairs made head and foot boards. The seats served as the sleeping area. There were two more chairs in the kitchen. He turned their backs to form the outside of his homemade crib. Out bed would serve for the other side. He stood back and grinned, then said, "Bring on the mattress, Mama."

"What mattress?" I asked.

"The one you're going to make with quilts if there are any extra ones around. Let's look."

We found three quilts that were not being used. Two were folded to make a soft resting-place for our babies. The third, folded, would serve as a covering. Not half bad, we smiled and congratulated ourselves.

We kept our friends' house and children more than a week. In that time Ewart cut down trees and sawed them into enough firewood to last the rest of the winter. I cooked and cleaned and washed clothes and sang fun songs and lullabies and loved six little children. We felt very much at home.

And on Sunday we took all of them with us to the church where my husband would preach that day.

IT TAKES A HEAP OF LEARNING AND A LOT OF LIVING

Backing Up To Go Ahead

There is an old adage that says, "Life can only be understood backwards, but it must be lived forward." That's what makes for adventure. Especially, if your heart is placed in God's keeping and your hand is on His arm and you are singing, "Help me, Lord. Help me, Lord." I was learning some things about the country, but I still asked myself, "What am I doing here?" The only answer seemed to come as the voice of God on the winds. "You are here because you have taken the first step in My assignment for you."

Steel Curls, Streetcars, and Model A Fords

In the city I was accustomed to various types of transportation. I could drive a car, call a taxi, ride a bus, or take a streetcar for seven cents a trip and go where I pleased. I did not give transportation a thought. It was just there, taken for granted, a part of my life.

I began my acquaintance with city transportation when I was nine years old. My father worked downtown. He was paid at noon every Saturday. Since my mother was ill for many years it became my routine to meet my father, whom we called Papa, and have lunch with him. With the money he gave me I would pay the bills and buy the groceries for the week. I loved it.

There was an added bonus. Not many nine-year-old girls had the pleasure of hanging steel "curls" in stringy, straight hair as I did. Papa was an expert machinist. Often he worked overtime on Saturday afternoons and I was free to roam the machine shop and pick up steel shavings where they had fallen to the floor. I hung them fancifully in my hair and dreamed of being beautiful. And in those moments, I was. Beauty comes from within, and beautiful thoughts bring inner beauty to the outside. I may never be that beautiful again.

As I tried to comprehend my new non-city life I looked backwards to the city life I knew so well. I understood it. I casually accepted it.

Not so in the country. Our city car was not built for country roads. Just as everyday living was more rugged than that in the city, transportation had to be also. We finally bought a tough old Model A Ford Sedan. It was so old and outdated that parts to keep it going were difficult to find.

At one of our churches a member in casual conversation mentioned that he had a Ford just like ours that he no longer used. To start it two wires had to be twisted together.

"What about the other parts?" my husband asked.

"So far as I know they're in pretty good shape, except for the lights. They don't burn," he said.

"How much would you want for it?" Ewart asked.

"Hadn't really thought about it," our friend said, "but I might take thirty-five dollars for it." We'd only paid $125.00 for the "good" one. Payments were $11.00 per month, and that was hard to come by.

"You've sold it," Ewart announced.

"You mean you want it?" asked the man, amazed.

"Yes, I do. We'll use it for extra parts for the one we already have," my husband told him.

"How will you get it home?" the man puzzled. "You can't drive both cars at the same time."

"I suppose he's thinking I'll drive it," I interrupted.

"Exactly," Ewart agreed. "Lola will drive behind me. Since it's almost dark, the lights of the front car will make way for both cars, and we'll do just fine." In my naïve way, I nodded.

After church we left in our separate cars. Ewart was driving the lead one, and I followed in the twisted-together-wires-starter one, without any lights.

Rash as this would have been in the city then, and in the country now, there was not as much danger as comes to mind. We were about twenty miles from home, traveling over dry dirt roads, and rarely saw another car in the many times we went that way.

We had backed up, car Model-wise, but we were planning on moving forward with the two of them.

A Hand Out and a Hand In

Learning is never ending, especially for preacher's wives. They constantly attend the "University of Life". Their subject of study one day may be Psychology, another—Business Management. Some days the class focuses on how to bring comfort to a person when you don't know what to say; and then at another time it may be simply to sit quietly and hold someone's hand. This kind of learning leans neither to the city nor the country. It is a universal learning that comes from books, yes, especially the Bible, but also from experience.

I learned a lesson one night about sitting quietly and

holding a person's hand. This lady was very ill. She had had no solid food in over three weeks and was now not even taking liquids. She refused them. She wanted to die. Her husband called us to come to their home. We went.

While Ewart talked with the man I went into the bedroom where his wife lay. She didn't move. She didn't speak. She showed no sign that she knew I was there. I sat in a chair next to her bedside and gently took her hand in mine. While her limp hand lay there I softly rubbed it with my other hand. There was no response.

Perhaps a half-hour later Ewart came to the door and nodded to me that it was time to leave. I leaned over my sick friend and said, "I love you." Then I was gone.

Three weeks later we had a telephone call. I was astonished to recognize the voice of the one whose hand I held that night. She sounded alert and there was a smile in her voice. "Can you and your husband come over and have supper with us tonight?" she invited. "I feel well enough to cook it."

"I'm sure we can," I answered. And we did. The sun was setting when we got to their house. The weather was warm and the couple was seated in the front porch swing holding hands.

In the middle of washing dishes after the meal she said, "Let's not do these dishes now. I want to talk with you." The men had gone outside to visit with each other (another country custom). She and I sat at the kitchen table. She took my hand, much as I had hers when she was so ill.

"That night when you came to see me," she began, "I wanted to die. I felt I had nothing to live for. My children were having no contact with me. They were too busy. My husband went about his usual ways. There was no communication between us. Sometimes we didn't speak all day. I became so depressed I couldn't eat, then couldn't even pray. I had cried until there were no more tears." She repeated, "I wanted to die."

"What helped you to get better?" I asked.

"You," she said. "It is all because of you."

I was totally dumbfounded! "Me?" I questioned. "I did nothing."

"Oh, but you did," she countered. "You sat by my bed. You held my hand and stroked it gently. And then, you said the words, 'I love you'." She patted my hand, then held it up and kissed it. "I felt that no one loved me. My heart was literally starving for love, and you fed me." She jumped up from the table, still holding my hand. "Let's go finish those dishes," she said. And we did.

I was still puzzled about one thing. She and her husband were holding hands as they sat in the swing when we arrived. What had happened there? She seemed to sense my puzzlement, and she laughed. "I know what you're thinking," she said. "How did I ever get my husband to hold my hand?"

I blushed as I admitted that was my thought. "I simply copied your example," she said. "I took his hand in mine, stroked it gently, and said, 'I love you'."

One Way to Brotherly Love

I had never thought much about the meaning of the word Philadelphia until I learned that its root word was from the Greek language and meant "brotherly love". I learned more about that meaning one Friday night when two couples from a church named Philadelphia knocked at our door.

To understand what took place after we invited them in, you have to know our circumstances at that time. We had no corner grocery store. Money was quite scarce and my husband refused to buy on credit except in an emergency. I'm glad he was that way. We would wait until after the offering given us at the church where he preached on the following Sunday before going to the grocery. We had enough food for us, but not for company.

Earlier in the day I had boiled some cabbage and made a chocolate pie that had no meringue because we had no eggs. This was to be our evening meal, along with a pone of cornbread. Not much, but we were making do with what we had on hand, and thankful for that—until the knock came at our door, and we had unexpected company.

That wasn't unusual for us. It happened often. As far as I was concerned, however, their timing was off. It was suppertime and I had no food to offer them except that cabbage and undecorated pie. I was very, very embarrassed, but I knew the polite thing I must do. They had seen our dining table.

Putting on my best fake smile I asked, " Have you had supper? We were about to eat. Will you join us?" Both women said, "Oh, we've eaten."

I said a silent prayer of thanks about that, but before I could add Amen my husband and the men came into the room. They had heard my question and their wives' answers. Both men spoke, "No, we haven't," they chimed almost in unison. I am sure that when they viewed our food offering they wished they had not spoken.

I thought back to my city days as a child. During the Great Depression navy beans could be bought for three cents a pound, a loaf of bread for a nickel, eggs were a dime a dozen, lard a nickel a pound and coffee a dime. That took a big hunk of money from my father's paycheck of $18.00 a week, but we were of the fortunate few. He did have a job.

There were ten of us in our household—my parents and grandparents and we six children, but we always had enough food for ourselves and for others. In the hill country where we now lived, the Depression had not totally given its last gasp.

Both men and women sensed my feelings, but before long they put my apprehension and fear on the run. We talked, we ate, and on Sunday our lovely guests told several people at church about their visit to their pastor's house, commenting on the warm welcome they received. My husband gave me a loving look that said, "See, I told you so. It's not what you <u>have</u> that matters. It's the way you handle what you have that makes a difference. If you show people you love and care about them, that's what they remember." For the rest of their lives, they and we were like brothers and sisters.

Still, embarrassing moments can be terrific teachers. I vowed that no matter what, I would never be caught again without some food on hand that could quickly be turned into a delicious feast. I have kept that promise to myself.

Crossing the Red Sea Would Be Easy Compared to Undoing What I Did

It was my first Sunday at a church my husband had just begun to serve. I was determined to make a good impression. I was happy to be there. I looked with appreciation at the large congregation, and I wanted to know each person individually. I am not good at keeping new faces and their names together, but that morning I had steeled my memory to do just that.

I was introduced to a woman who was seated at the end of a pew next to an aisle. I repeated her name as we met, and then marked it in a memory slot. On the other side of the aisle at the end of that pew I learned the name of the woman seated there. I followed the same procedure—name aloud—put it in a memory slot. I was confident that on the next preaching day the two women would be pleased that their new pastor's wife remembered each of them fondly.

Sunday morning came. The women were there, seated across the aisle from each other. I spoke to the one on my right first calling her by name then turned to the other. "How are you today, Mrs...?" She glared at me and said nothing. Then I noted that the first woman to whom I had spoken was red-faced and angry. "What do you mean," she said haughtily, "calling me by <u>that</u>—she shook her finger at me, then pointed across the aisle—woman's name? We haven't spoken in twenty years, and I don't plan to speak to her for another twenty!"

"That's right," the other woman spoke up, "and it will probably be twenty-five or more before I give her more than a cool nod. I'm insulted, even if it was in error, to be mistaken for her."

I apologized profusely. "I was so sure I had your names correctly," I said. "I don't know how I could have made such a mistake."

About that time the husband of one of the women came up. "Probably because they're on opposite sides of the aisle than they were last Sunday." He looked grimly at his wife, then back at me. "They're both good women," he said, "but just as stubborn as old gray mares." In my memory slots of the Sunday before I had never dreamed they would switch pews.

We stayed at that church several years. Each woman was nice enough to me if the other was not nearby. I'm not sure either would ever have forgiven my blunder had not my husband, a couple of years later, preached a sermon on forgiveness—on breaking the Alabaster Box of love on each other. That day this church began a new era. Those two women and I met at the church altar and God led us, through His Spirit, into His kind of love for one another. Just as God parted the waters of the Red Sea for the Israelites to cross over on dry land, so He had prepared the way down the Reconciliation Road.

THAT GOOD OL' COUNTRY COOKIN'

Do Country Preacher's Ever Tell a Lie?

I don't know about city preachers that may lie, but I'm sure I met one country preacher who did. I think he was trying to be kind, but he told a lie just the same. This happened about six months after we moved to the country, and it was all about cooking.

In the city I knew about electric cook stoves, gas stoves, and even oil-burning stoves. I never dreamed that in my new home I would be cooking on something entirely different. My stove turned out to be the fireplace. We didn't even have a stove. I looked at this new adventure thoughtfully and said, "This will be fun. It will be challenging, and I will be learning a new skill."

It really was fun, until we invited a local pastor to have dinner with us. I had planned a good country noon meal for him—green beans, boiled Irish potatoes, country sausage, a green salad, and cornbread. I knew he did not eat desserts so I didn't bother with baking a pie or cake. I hummed a merry tune as I went about my work.

The beans were boiling, the potatoes done, the salad

makings ready to be put together, the sausage in the skillet and the cornbread mixed. I could imagine how proud Ewart would be of the good meal we would offer our guest.

The man came early. His first words after the usual host greetings of "Hello. Come on in. How are you?" were: "I'm starving. When do we eat?" He and my husband had been friends since boyhood, so this type of behavior was one of camaraderie and did not seem out of place to Ewart. I was terrified. Dinner wasn't ready.

Hastily I added more wood to make a hotter fire. The sausage skillet was put on hot coals. The beans boiled furiously. The cornbread in its make-do oven rose beautifully while I mixed the salad and poured the potatoes into a serving bowl. In a matter of minutes we were seated at the table.

"You have some of my favorite foods here," our guest said. After giving thanks to God for the food, he served some of each item onto his plate. It did look pretty. The green salad with its red wedges of fresh tomatoes, the creamy white of the potatoes in their thickened broth, the browned sausage and neatly cut squares of cornbread made a handsome show. The green beans had a look of their own.

I was about ready to relax, smile, and enjoy a pleasant time. Then our preacher guest, who had eaten at the homes of many, many people, cut into his beautiful brown sausage. The cooked-too-fast sausage was raw inside. I cringed as he took a bite. He did not make a face nor lose his smile, but I lost mine. Next, he lifted some green beans to his mouth. They were so burned they looked like green-tinged, over-browned, stringy french-fries.

The disgusting meal was finally over. Our guest and my husband sat on the front porch and talked of their youthful days. I stood at the dishpan, washed dishes and rinsed them with my tears and had to do them all over again.

The time came for our friend to leave. He came to me, took my hands in his, and said, "That was a most wonderful meal. Thank you so much for it. I'll be back, if you invite me."

Do you think that preacher lied? I'm afraid I do. He did come back later and eat with us—after we got a cook stove. That stove caused our house to catch fire and burn down. It took nearly fifteen years for me to catch up to my city way of cooking. By that time electricity had come to our part of the country and I had an electric stove. What a wonderful treasure that was. As I used it I often remembered the kind preacher who probably told me a lie.

The Saga of Two Men and an Angry Woman

That Sunday was a beautiful day. We were in a small country town where Ewart was to be guest preacher at a weeklong revival meeting. We knew no one in the community other than the host pastor and his wife. As the morning service began the home pastor became ill and had to be rushed to the hospital. Before leaving he asked my husband to continue with all the services as planned.

The custom in rural churches at the time was that church members provide food for the visiting preacher and his wife. We had no idea where we were to eat at noon. Apparently the host pastor and his wife had been expecting us to be with them. Now, that was all changed. One of the deacons invited us to go home with him and his wife.

At their house the wife said to her husband, "Will you build a fire in the cook stove and get a bucket of water from the spring?" She and I went into the dining room to set the table.

In the kitchen my husband volunteered, "If it will help, I'll build the fire while you go for water." Our host grabbed a bucket and headed down the hill to the spring. Ewart placed splintered bits of pine knots on top of crumpled paper, and was about to strike a match when our hostess excused herself and left the dining room. She marched into the kitchen and walked toward the stove. My husband's back was to her. As he squatted in front of the stove's firebox she kicked him as hard as she could. "Why did you invite that preacher and his wife home with us?" she whispered in an angry voice. "You knew I did not have anything cooked!"

Just as she kicked, the back kitchen door opened and her husband, carrying the bucket of water came in. She looked at him, then at Ewart. "What have I done?" she cried and ran from the room. Her husband had seen and heard it all. He put down the water bucket and followed her. We heard him say, "If it will help your feelings you can kick me, too." With that, she got tickled. She gave him a swift but gentle kick. We all laughed, and the incident was put behind us. We had a lovely time. I helped with the cooking and the men washed the dishes and we were friends with a common bond. Both men had been kicked.

Biscuits Are Not Just For the Birds

At our house, until his death forty years after our marriage, my husband wanted and got freshly made biscuits three times a day. Quite often on Sunday evenings, after driving from a distant church, he would ask me to bake some biscuits, bring out the butter, and open a jar of home-canned peaches. This became a type of "comfort food" after a strenuous Sunday. If any biscuits were left over we crumbled them for the cardinals that came to our well house roof. They seemed to like my biscuits, and feeding leftovers to them became a daily ritual.

This went on for a number of years. On several occasions we received early morning food calls from the red birds. Their pecks on the window near our bed were similar to the army call, "It's time to get up. It's time to get up. It's time to get up in the morning."

One year on a cold, damp, March morning there came an almost shy rap at our front door. Darkness was so pervasive that I momentarily wondered if even the light of our kerosene lamp could penetrate it. The time was 3 o'clock. I thought of the beginning words of an old, old song—"It's three o'clock in the morning. We've danced the whole night through..." There had been no dancing at our house, however, and the light tap we had heard had been so unusual that it woke us. We knew there was no cardinal there. They didn't ask for food that early. This had to be a person. Ewart called out, "I'm coming," even as he tried to stick both feet in pants legs at the same time.

Today, anyone would be almost afraid to answer a door knock at that time of morning, but when the rap came at that long ago early hour there was no fear. Ewart recognized the man who stood there, and invited him in. Tall, rugged, still wearing a big portion of the tan he had received from plowing and planting and reaping in corn and cotton fields, he stopped inside. "I've come for breakfast," he announced.

By this time, I was dressed and came into the room and greeted our "breakfast" man. "As soon as the fire in the cook stove is hot enough," I said, "I'll be ready to begin cooking." We had learned by this time not to ask the why of the appearance at our door of unexpected guests. Sooner or later that would be revealed.

At the kitchen table, the two men talked of weather and crops and hunting and fishing. In the midst of a big fish tale, conversation stopped. Turning toward me our friend said, "Mrs. Autry, please let the cooking go for now and come sit with us. I want to talk with both of you." There was desperation in his voice.

The biscuits were in the oven, the side meat frying and the scrambled eggs almost done. The coffee had boiled. I pushed everything to the coolest part of the stove, pulled the biscuits out of the oven and set them on the open oven door and hurried to the table.

"I'm sorry I came to your door so early," he apologized, "but since my wife died hours don't seem to mean much to me. I can't sleep. I think of her all the time. I try to stop myself before talking out loud to her. I know she's not there in my presence, but somehow I feel as if she can hear me." He turned to Ewart. "Can she hear me, Preacher?"

"I don't know," my husband said gently, "but I do know that the Lord hears us when we pray to Him."

"I do that, too," he said. "I pray a lot. It's a big help. I don't know what I'd do if I could not pray, but I still miss her."

"Of course, you do," I agreed. A tear dropped from my eye. I wiped it hastily away. "You were blessed with a good wife," I said softly.

"Yes, Ma'am. I know she's in Heaven and that I will be there someday, too. Meantime…" For a moment he said nothing, then added, "I had to talk to somebody who would understand, and I know you and the Preacher do. Thank you."

The biscuits were still hot. The meat was crisp and tasty. The eggs were not too overdone, and the coffee was just right. We ate in almost complete silence.

The time came for our friend to leave. He gripped my husband's hand, then gave me a hug. Abruptly, he sat back down at the table. "I've got to tell you something else," he said. "Nobody in my family knows this but me. Not even my son." His hands were shaking as he took a sip of his now cold coffee. "I'm on my way to the hospital. I have to check in by eight o'clock. The doctors tell me I may never leave there. Will you pray with me and for me? I'm scared." We each reached over and held one of his hands. We prayed silently, then Ewart prayed aloud. After that our friend had to leave, to face whatever was the Lord's will.

Before he left he said, "Mrs. Autry, may I ask you a favor?" I nodded. "Will you wrap up for me those four left-over biscuits from breakfast? They taste so very much like the ones my wife used to make. I can eat them as I drive to the hospital, and they will be a comfort as I think of all the good and kind things she did."

On that cold March morning I realized anew that food is a part of living, but that true living is more than feeding the body. It also means feeding the Soul. Not everyone who asks for a biscuit is food hungry. He may need a listener-comforter even more.

And after that, he may be like the birds and want a biscuit, too.

Old Red, the Cow, Was As Patient As a Mule

Old Red was a cow loaned to us by a neighbor. We had walked four miles to his house and led her four miles back to ours. We had built a small pen and shed for her. The goodness of God to us was our main theme of conversation as we walked.

Milking a cow was as foreign to me as computers would be forty years later. My husband had milked cows since early childhood. It seemed natural that he would renew that skill with Old Red. It would be wonderful having fresh milk to drink. Rural stores of the time did not stock milk except as condensed or evaporated, in cans. The taste wasn't the same.

Ewart and I were rarely apart more than a few hours, but the time came when he was called to drive his brother to Louisiana. "What about Old Red?" I asked. "She will need milking, and I don't know how." I added, "We're having company for dinner tomorrow. You won't be here, and there won't be any milk for making bread. What will I do?"

He looked at me with that "you know what you'll have to do" look. It meant, "anybody can milk a cow if they just try." He wasn't trying to be smarty. I knew that. He was being practical. When something had to be done and you were the only one to give it a try, you pitched in.

"Tell me what to do," I said, "and I'll try."

The next morning at daybreak I picked up stool and bucket and headed for the cow pen. Old Red was waiting. Ewart had told me to get some feed and place it in a container for her to munch on. This was supposed to give me time to get my stool and bucket in place and begin the milking process. I was also told to watch her swishing tail. She could hit me in the face with it, or she could turn over the milk pail.

I sat down to milk. She gave one tail swish and moved a couple of feet. I moved feed, pail and stool and tried again. Each time she moved she took another step or two toward the gate which I had forgotten to close.

Outside the pen, she continued the process. She moved. I moved, carrying all the paraphernalia. We ended up at the back door steps. I cast aside the stool and took my seat on them. This time Old Red stayed, and with patience at my inept ability, chewed her cud contentedly. We had milk. I baked bread for guests and I thanked God for two things. First, that our adventure was successful. Second, that Old Red had patiently led me until our wills meshed. That's what God was doing in my life, also. Meshing my will with His.

The Wild, Wild Side

The wild, wild side of eating usually showed itself during the winter months. Gardens had long ago turned into barren, dry twigs. Once-flourishing rows of fresh vegetables had become like ghosts and left no signs they had been there. Those winter months were times of wild eating. I do not mean a wild orgy of food. I speak of foods from the forests, foods grown without being tended by man. Foods God has thoughtfully included in His wonderful world of nature. In some situations they might be thought of as survival foods. In our case, early after our move to the country, that is how we "made do" several times.

There was excitement and challenge in finding a balanced meal that was from God's own garden and was ours just for the taking—no tilling of soil, no planting of seed, no tending on a hot summer day. He had done the work. It was ours to preserve and use when the need arose. During the first days of May there were Spring Huckleberries to gather and can in sugar water, ready for a cobbler at a moment's notice. Dandelion greens also could be canned as well as Poke Salad. (Poke Salad is a wild, summer green that is poisonous if not prepared correctly, but tastes much like cooked spinach. Its stems can be made into pickles that are delicious, dilled or otherwise). Plums, muscadines, and wild grapes were used for jellies and jams. Wild strawberries and Fall persimmons added much in the fruit line.

In the meat line our woodlands were stocked with squirrels, deer, rabbits, ducks and a few turkeys. God had provided these, too. Our little creek had more fish than we would ever need.

So it was that one day during the bleak season friends from the city came to visit. In those days of few telephones in this rural area, visitors simply arrived. That was O.K. and expected. As I wondered what to prepare for the noon meal I thought of God's garden and meat supply. Aha! I thought. We'll have a wild dinner.

Their understanding of the word "wild" was not the same as mine. Theirs conjured up exotic, fancy foods. Imagine their surprise when they were served country-fried venison steak, wild poke salad greens and wild blackberry cobbler. WILD.

WISHY-WASHY WATER WISDOM

Scalybark Hickories, Lye Soap, Hot Bricks and Naked Blackberry Vines

We had been in our house in the country about a week when I realized some clothes washing had to be done. I did not know how. "Is there a Laundry anywhere near here?" I asked. "Nearly all our things are dirty."

Ewart said, "I'll have our own laundry set up by tomorrow morning. Don't worry." I didn't worry, but I did wonder. What did he mean—he'd have it set up? We had no washing machine. There was no electricity to operate one, and what about a dryer? I was totally confused.

The next morning dawned cold and clear. I missed him while I cooked breakfast.

Usually he sat at the table and drank a cup of coffee. Not this time. When he did come in, he was grinning. He bowed low. "Fair Princess," he said, "the laundry room is all set up. I'll help you with the washing."

A short while after breakfast he took me by the hand. "Let's take a little walk," he suggested. "Bundle up. It's cold outside." We walked down the bluff on which our house stood. In front of it there was a field that once had been planted in corn. Autry Creek ran along the far edge of it. A huge scalybark hickory tree stood a few yards from its bank. Another was about five feet away. Between them two wide planks had been nailed to form a low shelf. On it sat two new zinc washtubs. A brand new corrugated zinc washboard stood in the left-hand tub. A short distance from the shelf a black, cast iron wash pot—its three short legs resting firmly inside empty tin cans—was filled with boiling creek water, heated by a wood fire built beneath the pot. A cake of home made lye soap rested in a dry, brown oak leaf. The neatest item of this new "laundry room" consisted of two heated bricks on which to stand while washing the clothes. He had brought the soiled pieces and sorted them while the water heated in the pot.

I was amazed, amused, and anxious. How did anyone work this deal? I thought of just a couple of weeks before in the city. Then, hot water flowed into a washing machine. Washing powder was added. Clothes put into the water. A button pushed. That was it. At the end of the wash cycles, the clean garments were placed in a dryer. Taken out. Hung up. End of chore. But what now?

Ewart brought three buckets of creek water and poured into the tub with the washboard, then added enough boiling water to take the chill off the creek water. He took one of his white shirts, got it wet, placed it on the corrugated surface of the washboard, rubbed it with the lye soap, and began to move the shirt up and down over the rough surface. He paid special attention to the collar and cuffs. While he carried the shirt to the wash pot and put it into the boiling water I put other soiled white pieces into the tub and began to scrub them.

"Why do you boil these clothes?" I puzzled.

"All country women vie with each other to see who can have the whitest of the white," he said. "Boiling them helps.

Drying in the sunshine does the rest." He told me that his mother used to have a flat plank shaped liked a paddle. It was called a battling-board and was used to beat the dirt out of clothes.

As the white clothes boiled, the colored ones were soaped and rubbed clean, then put into the other zinc tub that was filled with rinse water. After the white clothes boiling they, too, were rinsed in clean creek water. During the entire laundry process as the bricks on which I stood cooled, they were replaced with freshly heated ones.

As fast as I put scrubbed clothes into the rinse water they seemed to disappear. I knew Ewart was doing the rinsing and wringing, but I hadn't a clue as to what he was doing with them after that. When the last piece was scrubbed and ready for rinsing he was not there. I turned to look for him, then simply stood still and gaped. The naked, leafless blackberry vines that rimmed part of the creek bank had suddenly blossomed. Springtime, in the guise of our wet clean clothes, decorated them beautifully. The wind could not blow them away, and the day was brightened.

A new adventure had been met head on, and I smiled. God makes everything so beautiful, I thought, even if it's just in the making of dirty clothes clean in His outrageously wonderful world.

Once Upon A time—
The Floods Came and So Did the Neighbors

Once upon a time the rains came, the waters rose and the land was flooded from hill to hill. The mighty Mississippi River was a gigantic, disastrous rushing sea, devouring anything in its path and swallowing it and disgorging it as it fled. I was twelve years old.

Although my family lived in a city that bordered the river, we were out of reach of its mighty roaring power. Not everyone was so fortunate. Cots for flood refugees were set up in schools and churches and other places large enough to house the victims. The people of the city opened wide their hearts and pocketbooks to care for them. Churches and pastors and others volunteered their help.

In spite of my age, I was pianist for a large city church. One afternoon my pastor called me. "Will you be free to play the piano at one of the refugee stations tonight?" he asked. "Our church is to have a worship service for the people of the flood."

I had never seen people who were hurting so much. Everything they had worked for had been swept away. Even the sandbags they had stacked higher and higher, to try to contain the waters in their natural course were moved, as if they had been filled with foam instead of sand. Nothing had worked. "I hope we can help them feel better," I whispered to a friend. Apparently, we did. They began to listen as we sang familiar hymns, then few by few they joined in. By the time the pastor spoke, tears were no longer visible. An occasional smile and a nod of heads in agreement with his words were signs of hope. When we left, there were hugs and thanks from many who just hours before had been wet and muddy and frantic.

The memories of that time came to me in a rush about a year and a half into our journey of living in the country. Rain had fallen for several days and the waters of the little local river were spread from hill to hill across the bottom-land. Autry Creek joined the river. Our house overlooked a vast flood ocean. Our car was parked on a rise about three quarters of a mile from us. As this "ocean" approached the foot of the hill it was hip-boot high in depth. My husband was bleeding profusely from a duodenal ulcer. There was no doctor nearby and no ambulance could have reached our house. Actually, there were no ambulances in our part of the country in those years. Doctors did make house calls, but there were no telephones available to call one.

The only way to get help was for me to walk a mile on a trail that led from the back of our house to a public road. On reaching that road there was another mile to go to get to the house of a neighbor who was at home. They had a car. We went to the closest town where there was a doctor. He gave me explicit directions for treatment. That was all he could do.

Meanwhile, another member of our neighbor family went to the community store and told of my husband's illness. Within an hour friends came to help. That help never lagged. However, Ewart did not gain health as we all had hoped. At the beginning of the second week six men, wearing slickers and waders (rain was still falling) came to carry my husband through the floodwaters to our car. They had brought a camp cot on which they gently placed him, covered him with a tarpaulin, picked him and the cot up, and started wading. I followed. We were trying to make it to the nearest small town where an uncle and aunt had invited us to stay with them until there was no longer a need.

As soon as Ewart was lying down on the back seat, and covered to keep him warm, the men literally pushed, pulled and lifted our car along the narrow mud road that was the only outlet to the gravel highway beyond the flood.

As I drove away I looked into the rearview mirror. I saw six good men standing at attention, hats off and held at chest level as if in farewell respect. Later one of them told me of their feelings at that moment. "We thought the next time we saw him we would be serving as pallbearers at his funeral."

This was not God's intent, however. Nearly two months later we returned home, and Ewart walked the now dry little road and up the hill to the house. God, in His gracious way, had given him health. He also had given me renewed understanding. It is not where you live, but how you live that is important. There are good and caring people everywhere. I thought of how God had protected Noah and his family during the Great Flood. He did not forget us, either.

Mud Pies, Water Pumps, and Joyful Singing

Most children like to play in the mud, to make mud pies and mud cakes. We were no longer children, but one rainy Sunday morning we knew we would be "playing" in the mud. Our destination was a new church building. The road to it was not complete. In fact, the way was narrow, and pure dirt; no gravel, no sand, no pavement; dug out with tractors along the tops of hills and across small valleys. Rain had fallen all night. The road was a mud quagmire. We stopped the car and got out just before the first mire would have buried our car to the hubcaps. With shoes, socks and towels in hand, rolled up pants legs, and held-above-the-mud skirt, my preacher husband and I began our trek to the church.

What an adventure, I thought. Mud went squish, squish, squish between our toes with each step. The mud was cool. The weather was hot. Sometimes we were more than ankle deep in the oozy stuff. Once we stopped and looked at each other, then burst out laughing. Along the way we sang the little chorus, "I was glad when they said unto me, Let us go into the House of the Lord."

Finally, we reached that little one room House of the Lord, but we didn't go in. We stopped at the house next to the church. There was a water pump in the back yard. Ewart moved the pump handle up and down until a stream poured out. I washed my feet, then pumped water for his.

When we entered the front door of the church the congregation was already singing the first hymn. At its close, the volunteer song leader, who also owned the water pump, quipped, "Well, Preacher, are your feet clean? We don't want any dirty-footed preacher trying to tell us what we should do." Of course, everyone laughed. Then he said, "We looked out the window and saw you and the missus using our water pump. That's okay. We'd rather have you borrow water than money." Everyone sang the next song with a smile.

A *"Crazy Man"* in a Wild River Bottom

The dawning sun pinked the blue-white snow still edging the riverbank. Patches of black earth showed through from white snowmelt and saluted in contrast. My husband had inched softly down the water's edge ready for the rustling sound of ducks rising for whatever it is that ducks do all day. He had heard their soft, chuckling, morning greetings to each other. Actually he did not care if he killed one, although we could well use the meat. He enjoyed being a part of an awakening world.

Duck hunting is not a hurry up and do it type of sport. At times it involves wading and standing in icy water for a long time. I enjoyed duck hunting because I enjoyed wading in water. My first experience with wading was in a mountain stream. I was twenty years old—on vacation. The water was soft and cool and caressing as it gently moved across my feet. I never forgot that. When we moved to the country and had to hunt for most of the meat we ate, I became enamored with duck hunting because of that one special moment of wading when I was still a city girl.

Ewart took a slow, quiet pace. This gave opportunity to look down the river as the sun cast early pastel shades over the water. He had not gone far. I knew this because I could hear him talking with another man. I heard the man say, "I think I'm losing my mind. Will you help me?"

I've never understood why, but it seems that some people are like magnets and draw troubled people to them. Ewart was one of those "magnets". Even in that vast bottomland a man in trouble found him. "How can I help?" I heard my husband say. "What makes you think you are losing your mind?"

"I hear children singing," the man said. "Why do I keep hearing children singing?"

"Because you are hearing children singing," Ewart told him. "They're my children."

"Are you crazy, too?" the man asked, almost with a sob.

"No, I don't think so," my husband said. "Come with me. I want to show you something." They walked together. "Be careful with your gun," he said to the man. "You're rather upset, and you don't need to become careless."

In a quiet, gentle voice Ewart talked to the man as he led him toward the campfire where our children and I waited. I had joined them in the singing. When the two men came in sight of the campfire they stopped. The stranger lay down his gun and with a gloved hand wiped his eyes. He turned to me and said, "Ma'am, your husband has just brought me back from the verge of losing my mind, and I thank him very much. But what are you and your children doing out here on a duck hunt before daylight when the temperature is below freezing? Aren't you afraid the kids will get cold and be sick?"

Our oldest spoke up. "No, Sir," he said. "We like this. We're not cold." He laughed before continuing. "We have on two pairs of everything and then we have this campfire." He looked up at the sky, then back at the man. "Did you ever see a shooting star? They're fun to watch. They're even better than the eggs and bacon we cooked on our fire here."

The experience of this man at the river made me think of Jesus and His love for the sea. A storm came as He and the disciples were crossing the Sea of Galilee. He calmed the waters, and His companions were safe. He, also, led my husband in calming the fears of the man who stood with us at our campfire.

Jack and Jill Had It Pretty Good

Jack and Jill may have gone up the hill to get a pail of water, but that wasn't to be for us. We had to go down the hill and lug the water up. My husband and I carried three-gallon buckets; the children had one-gallon molasses pails with lids so the water would not slosh out as they climbed. We measured the distance from the house—442 feet. Down hill or up hill, it was still 442 each way. The elevation from water source to water usage at the house was 85 feet. Many wells are not that deep. We had no well for two reasons. First, there were no shallow wells on hills like ours. Second, even one or two hundred-foot water wells at our location were almost unusable because of the iron content of the water. Spring water was pure and good, but like many things difficult to get in sufficient amounts to fill all needs.

One day my father came from the city to visit us. He had earlier given us some instructions: build a dam at the spring outlet that would allow the water to make a small pond three to four feet deep, get enough two inch water piping to go from the spring to the house. He did not tell us why but, after all, he was my father and we obeyed. Curiosity enfolded us. We had to wait.

When he came he brought with him a most unusual object—a hydraulic ram. "You'll have running water at your house before night," he promised. Again, my city education had given no knowledge of hydraulic rams. Ewart recognized the piece of equipment immediately. In his growing up days in the country, he had actually seen one in use.

My father was a hydraulic and mechanic specialist. I have no idea where he found that piece of "junk". That's what I thought it was—junk. It was about eighteen inches high. The cast iron upper part was a hollow globe resting on a small oval base that had two holes in it so it could be bolted down. There was a place for one spark plug, a gasket made of the tongue of an old leather shoe, and a hole where the first pipe would be fitted. I thought of all that 442 feet of pipe we had bought. There was no way this thing could work. It was rusty! I wondered if it were as nasty looking inside as outside. Apparently it had not been used in years. I learned later that these rams were mostly in use during the late 1800's and early 1900's. I wanted to cry.

My father and Ewart worked to install the ram at the spring pond; the children and I dug trenches for the laying of the pipes. By late afternoon we all gathered at the back door steps. A thoroughly scrubbed and sterilized 60-gallon oil drum which had a clean white cloth placed over the top was just to the left of the steps. We waited.

I had visions of a tap-size stream of water gushing into the container. Instead, when the water, pushed up that long hill by that tiny little ram, reached the drum the stream was matchstick size. My father was exuberant. "We did it," he shouted. Ewart's deep bass, "Yes!" joined in. The children clapped their hands. I just stood there. For a moment disappointment shrouded joy. Then, silently, I prayed, "Thank You, Lord. This is not the way I expected running water, but it is at the house. No more long climbs and heavy buckets."

The matchstick size stream filled the oil drum every twenty-four hours. Jack and Jill didn't have anything on us. Our water was at the top of the hill, too.

SNOWY AND ICY CURES CARRIED OUT IN CURIOUS WAYS

Old Tires Slip and Slide on Ice—Right?

Winter was upon us, and an overnight freezing rain coated everything upon which it fell. A cold sun created sparkles like diamonds in the ice. Tree branches, like traceries, highlighted the morning sky. God's awesome beauty could not be mistaken for the work of any other than He.

By the time of this ice storm, electricity had arrived in our community. We had become accustomed to it and its advantages. Now, ice coated power lines had broken and solid-iced trees had downed other power lines with their broken limbs and bodies.

We had not done away with our kerosene (then called coal oil) lamps, but there were other pre-electric things we did not hold onto that would have made life easier during the storm and its aftermath. We no longer used the hydraulic ram and its tiny stream. We had put an electric pump in the spring. We had done away with out wood cook stove. A gleaming white electric stove stood in place of the black cast-iron one. Electric heat had replaced the wood heater. There remained only the fireplace for warmth. All things electric were useless,

The first question the children asked that morning was, "What's for breakfast? How will you cook it?"

"Using the fireplace," I said, "as soon as your father figures some way to get us some water."

"He didn't come in and play Turtle with us this morning," one of the children said. "I missed him"

Turtle was a made-up game. Their dad would go from bed to bed acting as if he could not find the children. They would scoot under the quilts pretending they were turtles who had pulled in their heads and were hiding. When he went to the next bed, those he had already visited would poke their heads above the covers to peep out. They were ready to repeat the process until he finally "found" them.

We heard an outside noise and ran to a window. Oh, no, I thought. Ewart's gone outside and fallen on the ice. (Isn't it odd how we always think the worst before we learn the truth?) The truth was that my ingenious husband had solved the water problem. The noise we heard was made by buckets and pots being placed under the icicles hanging from the house eaves near the room where the fireplace was. That warmth would melt the icicles and there would be enough runoff to take care of needs other than drinking and cooking water.

Then he did what we thought was the most ridiculous thing we had ever seen. He sat down in the middle of an old automobile tire, an empty water bucket in one hand and a coil of rope in the other. He pushed off with his feet and skidded down the path toward the spring.

"How will he get back?" the oldest child asked.

"I truly don't know," I said. "I do know he can't stand up and climb the hill carrying a bucket of water. I also know he cannot slide up the hill seated in that tire. I turned to the others. "Let's be ready to help him if he needs us." We trooped to the porch all bundled in warm clothes, eyes fixed on the uphill path. We heard him before we could see him. He was singing, "Praise God From Whom All Blessings Flow." His deep bass voice echoed from hill to hill and reached us with assurance. He had tied one end of the rope around the tire, the other around his waist. The pail of water was anchored inside the tire, and with both hands he held onto bushes and trees and made his way to the house. We all shouted, "Hurray!" Then we joined him in "Praise God From Whom All Blessings Flow."

Lemonade, Sawdust, and Home Made Ice Boxes

One of the favorite summertime delights of many country people is lemonade made from fresh squeezed lemons. Often, for community get-togethers a scrubbed clean zinc wash tub is filled with water, sugar added, and halved lemons squeezed and left to float in it. Before the advent of electricity in our area, the only ice available was brought to homes weekly by the iceman. Quite a few families had iceboxes in which he would place 50 or 100 pound blocks of ice. Hunks of this were chipped off and placed in the tubs of lemonade to make it cold.

We were not so fortunate. We had no icebox, no place to put and keep ice for a week. Once in a while we did buy some, however. We tried wrapping the blocks in worn out quilts to keep the ice from melting as long as possible. This was not satisfactory. Just about the time we needed it most, the ice was gone. There was no way to preserve and keep food cold for any length of time.

Country people are noted for the ability to use what they have to create or make something they need. We had been out of the city long enough to pick up on a few things. One of these was that sawdust is an excellent insulator. Its main drawback is that it is so messy. On the hillside west of our house there had once been a sawmill. A giant hill of sawdust was still evident.

One Thursday we were expecting company from the city. That was also the day the iceman made his rounds. "I do wish we had an icebox," I grumbled to myself. "If we did, I could serve lemonade or ice tea." Then, resignedly, I pouted, "But we don't, and that's that."

A few moments later my husband walked into the kitchen and announced, "Honey, when the iceman comes tell him we want a 100 pound block of ice. We'll have our own icebox before he gets here."

I stood there, open-mouthed, speechless. I wondered— Does God answer the wants or needs of grumbling, pouting women even when they haven't prayed before becoming disgruntled? Ewart didn't give me time to ask his opinion on that question. His next words completely silenced me. "Tell him to bring it to the sawdust pile." I watched through the kitchen window as he picked up a shovel from a shed and walked away.

About an hour later he returned to the house. A look of "Hey, call me a genius" was written on his countenance. His first words were, "I did it. We now have an icebox." He stood tall, proud, and pleased. I didn't want to doubt him, but I had no clue as to how digging in a sawdust pile would bring about an icebox. He took my hand and led me to his project. There were piles of sawdust on either side of a huge hole from which he had dug it. "This is our icebox?" I stammered. He could not help but recognize my disappointment. The hurt of my rejection of his masterpiece was poignant. He looked like a little boy who had drawn a picture for his mother and she had made a wrong guess about what he had drawn.

His first joy of accomplishment had fled. Now it was up to me to bring some of it back. Quickly I tried to make amends. "Tell me how it works," I suggested. I tried to make my voice sound enthusiastic.

"It's a simple thing," he explained, "but I believe it will work. We can put a cardboard box in this hole." He gestured toward the dug out place. "The iceman will put the block of ice in the box, and I'll cover the entire thing back with sawdust. When we need ice I'll dig it out, chip off what we need, re-cover the rest and bring our ice treasure to the house. You can wash it off, and we'll have cold lemonade or ice tea whenever we want it. We might even make ice cream sometime."

By the time he ended his explanation I was as enthusiastic as he. "The iceman cometh today," I said. "Hooray! Hooray!" We clapped our hands and did a little jig in front of our icebox. We would not be embarrassed if our city guests wanted ice for their tea or lemonade.

We used that icebox for a long time before upgrading. Meanwhile, coming in from church one night a neighbor's cow, on the loose, ran straight in front of our car. We hit him dead center and he was dragged under our vehicle. We backed up. He staggered to his feet and walked on across the road. The impact cracked the engine block of the car. We got home in it, but it would never start again.

One day I noticed my husband looking in the trunk of that car. I watched as he cleaned it out thoroughly, brought several buckets of sawdust from the pile and poured them into the empty trunk. When he had enough he fashioned a new "icebox" that was nearer to the house and much more convenient to us and to the man who brought the weekly chunk of ice.

Eventually, when electricity became real in our part of the country, we had a Frigidaire, at that time the recognized elite of electric refrigerators. That was almost as important a day for us as when we bought a washing machine.

Meanwhile, I realized I was adapting to the methods of

my neighbors: do the best you can with what you have and don't make an issue of what you don't have—and I was glad. I looked toward the old car and to the sawdust pile. They had served us well. Was I serving the Lord where I was as well as these had served us?

Roofing Tacks, Old Shoes, and a Crosscut Saw

Ice was everywhere. Tree limbs were breaking from its weight and sounded like rifle shots as they snapped off the trees. I had experienced ice storms while living in the city, but since I had never heard the sound of a rifle shot I simply thought the limbs were breaking off and that was that. But, how much more interesting and to the point the description—like rifle shots.

By the time of this ice storm I had lived in the country long enough to realize that if I thought of each hardship as an adventure, tasks would be easier to work through and some might even be fun. I had learned to help with a two-person crosscut saw. That means there are handles at each end of the long blade. Two people work the saw by pulling it back and forth. There is a technique to using this kind of tool. If one sawyer puts a lot of weight on his end and the other doesn't, the sawing is very difficult. I had a good teacher, my husband. He taught me a new phrase, "Don't ride the saw." That means keep the sawing balanced.

The week before the ice storm we had cut trees, sawed them into firewood stick lengths and split larger blocks into quarters for easier handling. The problem we faced on that icy morning was that the wood was still where we had left it—on the second hill over from the house. There had been no time to haul it. Now there was no way we could do that. Our stash of nearby fuel would not last through the storm. This was an emergency. We had to do something quickly. Fortunately, we had not put the saw or the ax in the shed.

They were still on the porch.

As I cooked breakfast I heard Ewart whistling a merry tune. Then I heard the front door slam. "Surely," I said aloud, "he is not planning to try to walk anywhere." I went to the door and peeped out. He was standing on the porch, still whistling that same tune. In front of him was a line of old shoes, a pair for each of the children and us. A small bucket of roofing tacks was to his left. In his hand he had a hammer. I stepped out on the porch. "What are you up to now?" I asked.

There was a twinkle in his eyes. His nose and cheeks were red from the cold. I thought—if you had white hair, a white beard and a red suit you might actually pass as Santa Claus. *But I didn't say that.*

"I'll tell you after breakfast," he said. I knew he had an adventure planned.

"Bundle up and meet me on the porch," he told us when the last breakfast dish was washed.

There was a chair and a pair of shoes waiting for each of us. "We're going to try out a plan for having plenty of wood to last through this storm," he said. Then, eyeing the children, he added, "Without having to tote a single stick to be stacked. First person with the ice shoes on gets to go first."

We hurried. There was much debate between the children as to who won the "go first" right, but that didn't last long. We were too excited about being out of the house and doing something new. The shoes felt different than usual, tighter on our feet, but not uncomfortable.

"What did daddy do to our shoes?" one of the children asked. "They feel funny."

"I put roofing tacks into the soles, heads inside—points outside, to stick into the ice. Then I covered the tack heads with cardboard so our feet wouldn't feel them."

Ewart led the way, carrying the saw and ax. We carefully inched our way onto the icy hill road that rises in front of the house.

"We thought we would slide down, but we're not!" our daughter marveled.

Their father continued leading our climb, while singing a silly little tune with made up words: "I'm a genius. I'm a genius. Don't you agree? I'm a genius. I'm a genius, and my advice is free."

"What is your advice?" I asked. I sensed a lesson coming on.

"Be careful. You still might slide down, and then you would stop where our game ends."

"Where is that?" one of the children wanted to know.

"Wait and see," was the answer.

At a small flat spot on our uphill climb there was an oak tree. "This is where we stop," their dad said. "You children go far over there to my right. Mama, you and I are going to fell this tree and cut it into firewood, then the kids can come back and we'll have some fun."

He grabbed one handle of the saw. I took the other. As the tree plunged earthward the children clapped. One said, "Look, it had a million diamond icicles on it." The sun was out, and each icy particle acted as a brilliant prism.

"As we saw the tree trunk into short blocks," their dad said to the children, "your job is to get the logs to the front porch. See what you can do about it." For a moment they seemed stunned.

"But, Dad..." They spoke in unison as if they had rehearsed the words.

"Here's where the fun comes in," he told them. "Think about this. If you can come up with a plan to get the wood to the porch without having to carry a single bit of it, I'll pay you a nickel a block. What do you say?"

We went on with the work of sawing. They made no move for a short while. I said to Ewart, "Don't you think you should at least give them some ideas?" I felt sorry for the kids. They were small.

"I will," he said, "if they don't come up with a solution soon. I just thought this would be a good time for them to begin to learn to solve problems, and to have some fun, too."

The children were in a huddle much like the ones school basketball teams form. Suddenly they clapped their hands together. "We can do it," they cheered.

My husband and I stopped. We looked at each other. We were clueless as to their plan. We watched as each child lined up blocks of wood, one behind the other in the road, and angled them toward the house. With a little shove from a child, the sticks followed the icy road and rested against the porch. Not a one went astray. "Hooray," we shouted and urged the children on.

"This is going to cost me a pretty nickel," their dad told them, "but you've earned your pay." As the children passed by he gave each a hug. "You're great people," he told them, "and I love you."

"Me, too," I chimed in. "I'm so proud of you."

The remainder of the morning we worked and sang and had fun. Afterward, Ewart split each block into firewood size sticks and we stacked them on the porch. The children made up their own little song. "A block of wood plus a block of wood. And soon we'll have a pile. A nickel here, and a nickel there, and we'll be rich in a little while." It was almost as if they were teasing us, but we didn't mind a bit.

'S No Use, No Snow, No Ice Cream

The temperature was well below freezing. Long icicle spears, leftovers from a winter rain a couple of days before, hung from the house eaves. The ground was frozen, but there was no ice on it. The children had looked out the windows, hoping to see snowflakes, until they had about decided there would be none. "Let's go outside and play dueling with icicles," one said, and all agreed. They looked like snow bunnies in their heaviest winter garb. Moving around was harder and slower than they had first thought. There was little danger of harm with the icicles, but they soon tired of the game.

Their dad, sitting at his desk, looked up from his sermon preparing. "It's time for me to move around a little," he said. "I think I'll surprise them. Do you have an empty gallon size sorghum molasses bucket with a lid?"

"Well, yes," I replied, "but why do you want it?"

He grinned. "I want you to mix up some ice cream ingredients."

"In a molasses bucket?" I asked.

"Yep," he answered. "They've been good children all day. I think they deserve a treat."

"Aw, come on," I said. "You know there is no snow out there to make snow cream."

He looked at me, and teased, "Woman, I didn't say *snow* cream. I said *ice* cream."

"That's even more improbable," I countered. "We have no electricity, no freezer and no ice."

"Just mix all that stuff it takes for freezer cream," he laughed, "and stand by and see what 'mighty man' can do."

He picked up a three-gallon empty water bucket and went out the door. I stayed behind preparing the ice cream mix. "Help me get down a bunch of icicles," I heard him tell the children. "We're going to be eating *real good* in about an hour."

After being partners with their dad on many unexpected adventures, they didn't ask questions. They simply guessed and anticipated. "Now," he told the oldest, "go in and ask your mother for the gallon molasses bucket. It will be heavy. It has something in it. Don't drop it."

He centered the molasses pail inside the water bucket. The broken icicles were packed around and on top of it. Finally, he hung the buckets from a tree limb. "Let's go in, now," he said. "In one-half an hour we'll come back and see about it."

Rushing into the house they all asked questions of me. "What's in the little bucket, Mom? Dad said we'd have to wait, but we want to know now."

"I'm sorry," I told them as I rubbed warmth back into little hands, and touched their cherry-red noses with a wispy kiss. "You don't want me to ruin his surprise, do you?"

Like one, two, three the answers came, "Yes, Ma'am, yes ma'am, yes ma'am."

Instead of answering, I changed the subject. "How about helping me bake a cake?" I asked.

"Can I lick the cake batter bowl?" one after the other wanted to know.

"I'll leave enough in the bowl for each of you," I promised.

By the time the cake mix was in the oven to bake, their dad called, "Time to go outside." The tykes rushed out without even bothering to put on their coats.

About five minutes later they were back in the house. Their faces had lost enthusiasm. "What's wrong?" I questioned.

"Nothing. It wasn't any fun. We just turned that old sorghum bucket round and round and round, and nothing happened." Three more times they went outside and turned the sorghum bucket. When they came in the last time there were no smiles on their faces.

At that moment a Bible verse came to mind, "The Lord is good unto them that wait for him, to the soul that seeketh him" (Lamentations 3:25).

Sometimes it is so hard to wait. I had stood just a few days before in a similar situation as the children were now experiencing. I did not know what was going on. Nothing seemed to be moving as I thought it should, and as I wanted it. There was little joy in my heart. The children's problem was, to them, a big thing, just as mine had been to me. They had lost the joy of the results of anticipation. Their dad certainly wasn't God, but he was asking them to wait because he had something good coming up for them.

That is why God wanted me to wait, too. He had something good planned for me.

When Ice is King All its Subjects Bow Down and Burrow In

I suppose it is true that people who live in rural areas are more prone to notice changes in the natural elements around them than are city people. I am aware that is at least true with me. Many times in the city during ice storms my predominant thoughts concerned only inconvenience. In the country there was an acquiring of interesting facts and features.

Once after an extremely heavy snow and ice storm I took my camera and went out to see what I could see. I was amazed at the change in the shapes of things. Where bushes had been just bushes, they now looked totally different. One resembled a white poodle. Another, the letter T. A third could pass for a rare kind of giant bird. Other less predominant look-alikes took more imagination. All in all, this was a humbling experience—a natural phenomenon, yet one that must have made God smile.

There is a spot not far from the house where two hills face each other. I stood in the valley between the hills and looked up. I knew the layout: tall pines still green in spite of the cold, darker green cedars mingling like strangers in their midst, barren oaks with outstretched limbs reaching toward the sky. This day was different. Winter greenery wore a coat of white. There was a sense of awe and reverence. Even the wind was still, seemingly aware of something different. Silence was all around and in the midst of that silence—the head of every snow and ice-laden tree appeared to bow in reverence and awe.

I paused and bowed in prayer, too. Almighty God had again displayed His Majesty and glory and had accepted the obeisance of His creations.

PERSNICKETY
PERSPECTIVES

According to Webster's Dictionary the word persnickety means "unduly fastidious about trifles." Sometimes those trifles make for interesting outlooks and unusual happenings.

Table Trifles and Barnyard Surprises

One Sunday we were to have dinner with a family who had very little in the way of possessions. We did not want our young son to say anything about their circumstances. His father said to him, "Your plate may have a crack in it, or a plug out of it. Your tea could be served in a pint Mason canning jar because there aren't enough glasses for everyone, and there probably won't be a knife to go with your fork or spoon." He paused and looked into the boy's eyes. "It is important that you do not say anything about what they don't have. They are good people and they're trying very hard to make things better at their house. Do you understand, Son?" The child gave a solemn nod.

The table setting had been accurately described. The food was homegrown and very good. The host and hostess were gracious. Our son did not say a word during the entire meal.

About mid-afternoon he went with the man to feed the animals. This was a thrill for the boy. We left soon after their return and had driven only a short piece when he spoke for the first time. "Dad," he said, and he sounded as if he were puzzled. "I thought you said they were poor people."

"They are," his father said.

"But, Dad. I don't think they're all that poor."

"Why do you say that?" Ewart asked.

There was triumphant in the answer. "They've got two mules and a wagon, and that's more than we have."

Perspectives made the difference. To our child the table setting was of little consequence, but to have two mules and a wagon was awesome.

Ewart and I looked at each other. We had focused on trifles, but had been outdone by a child with a different perspective.

Dogs, Cow Hides, Rainy Weather and a Buck Deer

An outdoorsman neighbor—in our part of the country if you lived within one to ten miles, you were considered to be a neighbor—was meticulous about being prepared for any contingency when he went hunting. The first deer hunting season in the county since the early 1900's was about to open. Our friend and neighbor had made his plans.

Hanging on a barn wall was a tanned cowhide. Before daybreak on the first morning of that first hunt he took it down, placed it around his back, and tied it securely to his arms and legs. As he left the house his wife called, "Be careful. Someone might shoot you thinking you are a varmint."

"Don't worry," he answered. "Everyone in these parts is aware of what a cow looks like."

There was a light rain falling as he walked to the pasture

where he had seen deer playing the day before. The land was long and narrow, skirted on one side by the river and on the other by trees. He slipped noiselessly through the forest until he reached the place he had staked out as a deer stand.

Dawn was casting dreary, misty light and the rain was causing the wet cowhide to give off strong odors. Soon a deer moved quietly into the man's sight. The animal looked straight at the strange object, but apparently the cow smell was strong enough to quell any uneasiness. This was his time, the hunter thought, and he was prepared.

He dropped to his knees and began his stalk. His plan was to look and act like a grazing cow. In that way he could occasionally raise his head enough to keep the deer in sight but not make him suspicious.

When he was in close enough range he slowly raised his gun to shoot. The deer had paid the "cow" no attention.

In his mind the man was already accepting the applause of fellow hunters when he brought in the deer. He was exulting in their praise of his imaginative and careful preparations. But these things were not to be. At the moment he would have pulled the trigger there was an intruder. His cow-herder dog had spotted the hide and knew no cow was supposed to be there. The strong smell of the wet hide overpowered the human odor. The dog did exactly what he had been trained to do—grab a cow by the heel to cause it to go in the direction it should. The cowhide-covered master received the reward of his dog training. The deer fled when the hunter yelled. So did the dog.

This great hunter untied the hide from his arms and legs, flung it aside and walked away, disgusted. He had been particular about the little things, but he forgot the most important—to make sure his dog could not follow him.

I learned a lesson that day, too. We often major on the little things of our lives. We forget that all our details are as nothing if God has to nip our heels to remind us of Who He is.

Gasoline, Rotten Eggs, and God's Providence

The old open-sided Ford touring car, its winter ising-glass window coverings removed for the summer, pulled up to the gas pump at our neighborhood store. A man and woman got out. She carefully cradled in her hands a paper bag. In it were twelve hen eggs. The couple were sharecroppers. The landowner for which they worked supplied their needs and gave them a place to live for the year. At harvest time, their bill for the year was calculated, expenditures taken care of, and cash payment for their work paid them after all adjustments had been made. Many times during the era of the end of the Great Depression sharecroppers had very little money and had to go right back into debt with the boss.

This was the situation in which this pair found themselves. They had no money. They needed gas for their car. Their solution was to see if the storekeeper would put a gallon of gas in the car in exchange for a dozen eggs.

The storekeeper knew the couple. He explained to them that even though gasoline was fifteen cents a gallon, eggs were only ten cents a dozen. Sadly they turned to leave, not knowing if they could even get back home in their car. The woman was crying.

As they stepped off the front porch of the store a man walked up to them and spoke. Before he even noticed she was crying he said, "Hi, neighbors. I've a question for you?"

"Not now," the woman said, and she sobbed.

"What's wrong?" the friend asked, and she told him about the gas and the eggs.

He began to smile. Then he laughed out loud. She and her husband were startled. This man had always been kind and friendly. Now he was laughing at them in their troubles.

"Excuse me," she said. Hurt accompanied her words. She began to walk away.

The neighbor called to her, "Wait! I'm not laughing *at*

you. I'm happy *for* you. Look on top of your car."

A canvas canopy served as the top of the car. From where she stood she could not see the car roof. Her husband could. He broke into a run, stretched himself for a good view, and shouted, "Honey, God's done it again!" There was a distinct swag in the center of the canopy. In it were eighteen eggs a hen had laid for a setting.

The storekeeper, knowing the eggs were probably too old for him to sell, nevertheless took them and the first dozen as payment for *two* gallons of gas.

God sometimes leads us into little adventures that speak louder than words.

It's All In How You Look At It

Two children stayed in the car in front of a liquor store while their mother went inside. No, she was not going for liquor but in hopes of getting some cardboard boxes in which to pack things. Her parents were moving and she was helping in the process. She had been told they had some new crates they planned to discard because they were in the way.

As the children waited, the younger one, age three, spoke to his five-year-old sister. He had never heard of a liquor store and wondered what it was. "What's a liquor store?" he asked.

His sister thought for a moment. She didn't know, either, but she felt compelled to give him an answer. "You know," she said. "It's a place where you lick things."

Wrong answer. Good reasoning, if you are simply listening to a word—"liq-our" (lick-er)..

I knew a pastor who almost got into trouble with his church because he once went into a saloon. He was walking down a street and as he passed the place, glanced in the window. At the same time a man seated inside, drinking a beer, saw him. The man beckoned for the preacher to join him.

For some time the pastor had prayed for this man. He, through the use of alcohol was hurting himself, abusing his wife and children, and about to lose his job. This preacher went in, knowing that if members of his congregation saw him there they would come to wrong conclusions. He knew God wanted him to do this.

The drinker offered the pastor a drink. "No, thanks," the preacher said, "but I will let you buy me a Coca Cola." They sat and talked—one drinking alcohol, the other a soft drink. Finally, the question was asked, "Preacher, why did you come in here? Have you ever been in a place like this before?"

Answering the questions from last to first, the pastor said, "No. I've never been in a place like this. I did not want to come in. I did so, because God loves you and He sent me to tell you that."

I would not be truthful if I said the man immediately surrendered his life and his will to the Lord. I can tell you that several months later he surprised everyone by coming to church. A short time later he told this story to the congregation, as he became a follower of Christ.

"Where He leads me I will follow."

The Old Man Was in Love

Several years had passed since his wife died, and he had once again fallen in love. Every day he passed by his beloved's house. Every day he stopped. Every day she waited for him at her rural mailbox. She had never married, but now she had found her true love, or to be more exact, he had found her, and life was beautiful. Finally he proposed and wedding plans were made.

My husband was to perform the ceremony, but it was not to be in the church, but rather on the side of a main highway. The prospective groom had chosen the spot for its sloping beauty, culminating as a high hill. Its location was the border between two states. My husband was licensed to perform marriage ceremonies in both states, so the man had his choice of which side of the border line he and his bride would stand. His reasoning was that he wanted his sons who lived in one of the states and his new wife who lived in the other to become as family; to be comfortable with one another and in each other's homes.

The sun was shining on their wedding day. They stood on a small almost flat place near the hillside, facing the highway. My husband stood in front of them and began the ceremony. Only a few seconds into it the groom said to my husband, "Wait a minute. Don't say anything else."

"What's wrong?" Ewart asked.

"I'm standing on the wrong side." He moved. His bride smiled. "Now, go ahead," he ordered.

Ewart began again, "Dearly beloved, we are gathered here to witness…" Again he was stopped. "What's the problem now?" he asked.

"No problem," the man replied. He then pointed down the highway. "Do you see that man mowing the grass on the right-of-way? Well, he's a friend of mine. Let's wait until he comes closer. I want him to witness this."

When the friend was within hearing distance the groom began to wave his hand and call to him. "Get off that mower and come over here. I want you to see this well done." All this time he was holding the hand of his almost legal wife. She knew him much better than we did, and understood his behavior.

The ceremony was begun once more and was finally completed. The man and his new wife took off on their honeymoon, and lived many happy years.

We saw them often through the years and I had thought of the happiness of the groom, the patience of the smiling bride and the persnickety way the man had behaved. Every detail was of vital importance to him. He wanted all to be perfect. At the time I had wondered about it, and about how his new wife truly reacted to his seemingly inane mannerisms. I learned the answer a few months later.

He called us one morning. "Can you come to our house about two-thirty this afternoon?" he asked. We told him we could. When we arrived he led us through the front door, then out the back door. As we walked, he explained.

"My wife and I have rented the little house behind ours to a dear lady," he said. "She is a widow, has very few possessions, and is not a Christian. Can you help her?"

"I don't know," my husband answered, "but we'll be glad to visit and talk with her, and see what we can do."

"That's what I wanted you to do," he said.

When we reached the halfway point between the two houses, he stopped. "Let's stand here and talk a few minutes," he said. "I didn't tell her you were coming, but she knows you're here. I saw her pull back the curtain a slight bit and peep out."

We didn't know what he wanted to talk about. Actually, he said he did not care about what we said. He simply wanted us to appear to be in conversation. We stood there probably five minutes, chatting about this and that and nothing that mattered. Then he said, "Let's go. She's ready for us now. Her hair will be combed, she will be wearing a fresh apron and she will not be embarrassed."

The man's desire for perfection was not rooted in self-centeredness, but in thoughtfulness, in the desire to make whatever the occasion, the happiest and most memorable possible. We had a happy, relaxed time with the lady. Good came from the visit.

Back at our host's house, his wife asked, "How did it go, Honey?"

"Perfect, Sweetheart," he said. "Just as we prayed it would."

The old man was not only in love with his new bride. He was in love with God, too. He had also done me a favor. His behavior was thoughtful and Godly. I realized I wasn't consistent in either of those behaviors. I strongly felt the need for forgiveness of the times I had simply rushed into situations and taken over.

PART THREE

THE ACCEPTANCE

ADVENTURES IN FOLLOWING

City Life Versus the Call of a Whippoorwill

Even if God's will *is* first in our lives, this does not negate remembrances of things we have loved. I was eagerly looking forward to a planned trip to the city. Early Spring had brought cool, crisp, sunshiny weather. The oak trees bore their leaf buds. Other kinds had teenage leaves. Flowering trees were displaying their pastel blossoms. I wore my new outfit. My husband never looked more handsome. Life seemed as promising and vibrant as springtime.

We were to attend a national meeting of Pastors, their wives, and other church related people. Some we had known for a long time. Others would become special friends. We sang as we traveled. What a special time this would be!

We attended the first morning meeting as scheduled. During the after-lunch break we went downtown. The window gazing I had missed so much was waiting. I might even buy something. I was like a kid with an ice cream cone on a hot day. I could "taste" the pleasure of trying on high-heeled shoes.

In the midst of my enjoyment there came a sense of something missing. My thoughts would not stay focused on shoes and clothes. The clamor, the noise, the rushing of pedestrians to cross the street before the lights changed, the blank stares or the unawareness of human being to human being began to make the sound of Autry Creek become an almost whispering, agonizing memory. The lure of the city was not the same for me as it had been. Thoughts of the little house our neighbors and church people built for us shortly after ours burned were reminders of something that was missing on the city streets. Everything was rush, rush, hurry, hurry. Except for tight little groups of people, mostly teenagers, there were few smiles and even less laughter. There was a difference that was almost palpable in the sense of neighborliness and caring that was so prevalent in the slower approach to life; a sense that had intensified and brought comfort and security even in those hard days of the past.

There are many good, caring, sharing people living in cities, but because of a multitude of factors there is an aloofness that prohibits general geniality. I found myself becoming more like my fellow pedestrians than I cared to admit. I barely noticed the young mother struggling with her small children. The old man seated on a downtown park bench almost spoke, but we passed him by.

However, it was the song of a bird in a city park that finally brought about my acceptance of country life. I firmly believe God opened that little bird's mouth when I was near enough to hear it. I also believe His message through that bird was, "Go home—to the country. Be content there until I show you another way."

I turned to my husband. "Let's go home," I said. "I want to hear the whippoorwills call tonight."

Follow the Rabbit

When winter blahs, due to staying in the house too much, became almost unbearable our family had a sure cure. Follow the rabbit. Any rabbit. First we had to find one, then flush him out of his hiding place. As he scampered through the snow we applauded and watched him go, but we felt sure we would see him again. We were playing "Trackers". This is a game in which there is no catching or killing of a quarry. You simply try to follow the trail left by the animal. Since we could not do this by scent like a bloodhound, we waited for a snow deep enough for a rabbit to leave footprints.

One morning we awoke to a four-inch overnight snow. "This is the day?" each child asked after a quick look outside. "No school," one said. "Rabbit," another promised as he looked through the window toward a briar patch in which one sometimes hid, "today we will find your secret hideout."

A cold sun lit a path across the snow. We began our trek, first to the briar patch, but no luck. The children ran and laughed and slid down snowy hills. Occasionally they pitched sneaky snowballs at us. We didn't mind. This was a day of making memories.

By noon we had not seen a rabbit. The children were beginning to be hungry and a little cold. We knew of a nearby overhang of huge rocks that would make a good camping spot. There was no snow under the rock ledge. Close by were pine knots. Back in my city days I would not have known about pine knots, but now I was thankful for my new knowledge. Pine knots are just what the name implies—knots of pine, rich in turpentine, that have hardened after the death of the parent tree. The main part of the tree might decay but I never knew of a pine knot losing its shape or substance. I have learned since moving to the country that they are good for starting fires, for using as flares, and also as light along dark pathways.

It seems that Abraham Lincoln knew about them, also. The story is told that he studied his school lessons by the light of pine knots. He probably built a fire in the fireplace with one or two of them when needed. They create intense heat as they burn. Pine knots were very valuable to those who had to start fires in wood-burning stoves or fireplaces. Sometimes, before winter set in, families combed the woods gathering them for future use. We set about digging under the snow gathering some for our wintry picnic.

We had great fun huddled together, warming hands and feet by the fire, sheltered from wind and snow and eating the food we had brought with us. We enjoyed our little hideaway for perhaps an hour—until one of the children peeped out. "There's a rabbit watching us," she whispered.

Hastily we put on shoes, socks and gloves, put out the fire and began following the rabbit's footsteps. I am fully aware that rabbits don't play the game of "catch me, if you can", but this little fellow seemed to understand that we were not planning to harm him. He ran a short distance, then sat in the snow as if waiting for us to get in sight. When we did, he moved just beyond our vision, sat down and waited, and moved on as before. He didn't run scared as if being chased by beagle hounds. We talked about it and agreed that he enjoyed the snow as much as we did.

Finally we found his hiding place. He sat there, looked at us, and did not move. We knew the game was over.

Back in our own little house I thought about the day. How did that small, furry creature know we meant him no harm? Does God give animals certain degrees of instinct that reveal such things to them?

Does God deal with us in degrees as we seek to follow Him? Does He stop and watch our progress? Had He done this to me? Was He showing me He had confidence that I would move from struggling over city-country comparison?

That I would survive feelings of inadequacy and ignorance? That being poor materially was of much less importance than spiritual poverty? That, even though I had far to go, He was at this time pleased with my progress?

Was He showing me that even, as that little rabbit had shown confidence in us when he led us through the snow, I should have utter confidence in Him and His plans for me?

Follow the Children, Too

Honesty is their name. They tell it like it is. The Bible says in Isaiah 11:16 ..."and a little child shall lead them." I might say they lead in most unusual ways.

My daughter-in-law was teaching a group of Special Education Students. One little girl, in particular, had her own charming way of expressing herself. One morning she arrived at school early. She had brought her new walkie-talkie. When the teacher entered the room she heard a voice behind the door carrying on an animated conversation with someone. "Yes, Sir," the little voice said, "I'm at school." After a pause, "No, Sir. I'm not in trouble. I just wanted to call somebody." Apparently the person with whom she was talking asked how she happened to reach him. "I just punched some buttons and you answered," she said.

My daughter-in-law, the teacher, walked behind the door, gave the child a hug, and said to her, "Honey, let me talk, please." She explained who she was and the circumstances, then said, "May I ask who you are?"

He chuckled and replied, "I'm the County Sheriff."

That little early morning adventure brought to mind another learning experience from this same little one. Dessert for school lunch that day was chocolate pudding. The weather was warm and so was the pudding. Eagerly this small student put her only eating utensil, a fork, into the pudding. As she tried to lift the food to her mouth it slid off the fork. After the third or fourth try she began to cry. She watched again as the same thing happened. Then with tears in her eyes and a sob in her voice she said almost prayer-like, "Please come back, Pudding. Please come back."

How like me, I thought. The right person, my Lord, is always ready to talk with me. He is also prepared to answer my prayers when I've tried all I know to do, and ask for His help. He even calls, "Please, come back. Please come back."

Told Like It Is

My seven-year-old granddaughter wrote an essay about me. For her work she received the first place award for Grade 1 students of all the schools in her city. I am proud of her ability. She is carrying on a family tradition of writing. Her mother and aunt and grandfather and great-aunt and great uncles and great-grandfather and great-grandmother and several other relatives are published authors.

However, the honesty of her writing is the thing I admire most. I've been teased a lot about what she wrote, but I've had a whole heap of fun with it, too. Her honesty, as she tries to follow the directions of her heart is refreshing, and I am encouraged to follow the ways of mine also for, I believe, both are of God.

Her essay, included in this book with her permission and that of her parents, follows:

"My Grandmama and Me"

On Thursday when I come home from school I really want to go kerplunk on the couch and watch T.V. but I have to kerplunk right on the peano bench. My great-grand-mother teaches me peano lessons. She has short white hair and blue eyes and she can even take her whole jaws of teeth out! My daddy says she's 88 or something high up in the ages. For a old woman she's oh so smart! She tells me what notes are on the peano and she tells me to sit up strate and hold my hands in reddy posishun. I am learning lots of things I never knew I could do—like playing Deep and Wide. I love to watch T.V. but I love to spend time with my grandmamma a little bit better! I love you Grandmama!!"

Lord, help me to be as honest in my life as my little great-granddaughter is in hers—Please!

The Table

We were not at home when our house burned. Everything was lost except the car and the clothes we were wearing. Our neighbors built the one I now live in (there have been additions and alterations since), but we had no furniture. For a short while my husband and I used a rough-cut, fifteen-inch wide cypress plank for a table. We placed it across a corner of a room and anchored it on two windowsills by lowering the bottom sash of the windows onto the plank.

However, when our family increased we decided to have a built-in table with benches on each side. The table nook was cozy-near to the wood cook stove, and on cold evenings the children did their school homework on that table. It was a little like being "snug as a bug in a rug". They loved it!

As economics improved, so did our finances. One day Ewart and I decided the time had come to get a nice table. We mentioned that thought to one of our church members. He immediately said, "I have just the thing for you. It has been in my barn loft for twenty years. It had belonged to my brother, and it became mine when he died. I had no use for it, but it was too good to throw away. You can have it for nothing, if you want it."

The table was beautiful. Round top, round pedestal base, two extra table leaves to enlarge the table size when needed, and all of solid oak. The man apologized about one flaw he had noticed. Near the center of the table was the imprint of a "smoothing iron". When I lived in the city I had no idea what a smoothing iron was. I soon learned. It was used to press wrinkles from clothing just as modern irons fulfill the same purpose. The difference in the older and new types of irons is that the older ones had to be heated either on a stove, or on hot coals of fire. Apparently our friend's sister-in-law used the table surface as an ironing board. Somehow the iron was so hot that it burned through a pad on which it had been placed, and left its imprint on the tabletop

"You can sand the top down and maybe the burned spot will come off," the man suggested.

"I may refinish the table," I told him, "but I don't want to take the iron mark off. To me, that mark is a symbol of the past."

We brought the table home. The children were delighted until they learned we were going to take down the home made, rough plank one that stood in the corner near the stove. They began to cry. "Please don't take *our* table down," they begged. "We love it. That's all we've ever known."

They cried as we ripped away at the unsightly boards, and I felt guilty. We were removing a landmark in their lives. A landmark that stood for security, and warmth, food, fellowship and love. Many times I have wondered if they had ever read the Scripture that says, "Remove not the ancient landmark, which thy fathers have set" (Proverbs 22:28).

I realize this is not speaking of tearing out old tables, but when I understood how we were removing something they treasured very much, I knew I would miss the closeness we had all felt as a family in that special spot. And I cried, too.

God leads through happenings, events, and adventures. I have thought of that table many times. I have used its story to illustrate the landmarks of our lives and how God so wonderfully incorporates his Word into those times.

KISSIN' COUSINS

Since Eve Was the First Mother,
Where Does That Leave Us as Cousins?

Kissing cousins are those who, no matter the actual distance away from being "first" cousins, always greet each other with a kiss. Most of the time it lands on a cheek, but not always. At times that kiss lands square on the mouth, and it is never forgotten. I remember a special one I received when my granddaughter and I were in Russia on a mission trip.

We had met some very wonderful Christians. They had kept their faith in Christ alive for many years under very severe restrictions. The pastor of the church was imprisoned fourteen years because he was committed to telling others about Christ. There were other stories that varied in detail but all pointed to a deep, solid belief that Jesus is their Savior.

One woman was a doctor. I don't know her story, but since she was at least middle aged I presumed she had been a member of the underground Christian community. Many times when I pray, I think of her. At almost every service she was asked to pray for everyone present. She did not stand, as most in our country do. Rather she moved to the middle aisle and knelt. Her prayers could not be held back by threats or by time, or roofs over buildings. I've heard some Christians say, "I feel as if my prayer did not even reach the ceiling." There was a sense, an awesome feeling that made this listener and co-pray-er aware that the doctor had a straight line to God's throne. Her face was lined, and hinted of things she would not tell, but I believe she was in direct contact with the One Who knows all things.

The family with whom we lived while we were in Russia was fortunate enough to have a television. One day we came home to find them clustered in front of it. An American pastor was preaching. His message was being translated into the Russian language. As we entered the door one of the women gave us a quick glance, put her finger over her lips, saying in effect, "Please don't say anything. We don't want to miss even one word that he says." We recognized the preacher, but it was we who did not understand the message.

With that family we became Christian kissin' cousins.

However, it was on the last day for our mission work that I received the lip kiss. We were soon to leave, and we were saying our good-byes. One of the ladies came shyly up to me. She put her arms around me and hugged me tightly. "I'm one of nine children," she said. "My father was an underground preacher. He held secret services in our home." Her voice quivered and she began to cry. Then she said, "When I was fourteen years old, those who opposed Christ came. We were not surprised, but we were terrified and sad. They took our father away. We never saw him again."

It was then, at that moment, that she kissed me full on the lips—not the casual kiss on the cheek of greeting or goodbye, but a kiss that told a story. "In spite of all that happened to us because of our faith," she said, "I still love Jesus. She added, "I love you, too, because of HIM." We were, indeed, kissin' cousins in Christ.

Water Skimmers, Deep Divers, and What's Next, Lord?

One of the great imagined inventions for which I would like a patent is a pair of shoes that would enable one to walk on water as easily as on land. Not some big, cumbersome outfit. Just ordinary looking shoes with built in buoyancy. Perhaps someday someone will claim that patent. I have not earned it yet.

I read recently that the secret of walking on water had been uncovered. The secret is: to be born of a Virgin birth with a star of your own in the east. That is how Jesus, God's Son, was born. Because of Who He is, Jesus was able to walk on water. The disciple, Simon Peter, tried and failed. I have, however, seen a tiny creature that walks on top of water. I watched one do that, and he seemed to be having a wonderful time. Skimming along like an ice skater, or walking with a pushing movement of his middle legs, he guided his direction with the back ones. This insect is appropriately named Water Strider or Water Skimmer. It also has another name—"Jesus Bug." Where did that title come from? The fact that Jesus walked on water, and so does this tiny creation of His.

This bit of facetiousness about a name has nothing to do with the Water Skimmer's ability to walk on water. It has much to do with the ability of God's children to carry out His plans for our lives. God gave this small insect what was needed for its well being. He has given us much more. The Skimmer only touches the top of the water, never reaching into the depths of his world to explore or analyze or think. God left that to mankind. We, however, are more like the Skimmer than the explorer. It is simply easier to skim a Scripture, give a few dollars to a charity, say a hasty prayer than to reach into God's Word, know what it says, and do it with passion, understanding and thought.

One of the great adventures of walking with the Lord is

that He shows His followers the depths of His Word, the wisdom that is available, the joy and peace that come from obedience, the security that He offers.

I came home from my encounter with the Skimmer vowing that no matter where God placed me I would accept and fulfill His purpose for me. This is not easy. At times there are things *I* want to do, places I long to see. God understands this and often lets me have my way. At other times this is not His plan for me. It is then that temptations burst forth like fireworks on a hot July night. Excuses, not reasons, abound. Self acts up. God reminds me of The Skimmer, and I am subdued. When I have renewed my vow, when His will and mine are close like kissin' cousins, He forgives and leads to a new adventure walk with Him.

Kissin' Cousin Toothbrushes and Other Everyday Objects

I was visiting in the home of friends who had served as missionaries in West Africa. They showed many objects made and used by members of the tribe with whom they worked. My friends had used them also. Among the artifacts were a toothbrush, a comb, a food mixer and a calabash. My friend said, "Toothbrushes are made from lemon trees. The people cut off pieces of small limbs about the size of a yellow pencil and half as long. They chew on one end of the stick until it becomes like a small brush. That's the end they use. Something about the wood makes their teeth very white.

"Hand made combs are carved from a very hard red wood (mahogany) by talented craftsmen. It is called 'bois rouge' which literally means 'red wood'."

My friend showed me a comb she had brought with her from West Africa. It was like a hair pick that can be bought here in the stores. These combs usually have several very sharp, four-inch long teeth and short handles. Both women and men use them. The ladies use porcupine quills to do their hair, too.

She picked up something that looked like hay, and handed it to me. "A washcloth is usually a wad of dry grass that has been pressed together in a pad or piece about the size of your hand," she said. "They wet it and scrub themselves with lye soap to become clean." The washcloth resembled our loofahs.

The next item was a food mixer. "It's a limb from a small tree," she said. "The limb chosen to make it will have about 5 smaller limbs in a cluster. They cut the smaller limbs off about two inches from the end of the larger limb and leave the larger limb about eighteen inches long. The large limb is rubbed between their hands to make the 'mixer' turn."

Then she brought out a large gourd. It was hard and smooth on the outside. "This is a calabash," she told me. "

"Do they grow these?" I asked.

"Not really," she replied. "They go into the forests and find them growing wild on vines that climb bushes and trees. They cut the gourds in half, clean out the seeds and other contents and use the gourd itself for many things. Calabash bowls are used for serving food, carrying things on their head, mixing foods, dipping water, or whatever else they have need of using a large bowl. The ladies who work the rice fields take their food to the fields in a calabash with a cloth tied around it. After they eat the food for the day, they sometimes use the calabash for a hat, especially if it begins to rain."

Other created objects from the world of nature around the tribe included pot scrubbers made of grass, washboards and delicate artwork. The tribal village was far from a town. There were no stores, yet their needs were met.

I marveled at the ingenuity of that tribe. Many of their household utensils bore the same names and were used for the same purposes as those we have. All were fashioned from natural things that grew around them. I also became aware of the ways our cultures are so much like kissin' cousins. Related, but not the same. Worthy and useful, each in its own place. Not all look, act, or speak alike, but each has a God-given purpose.

I'm still working on mine.

Almost "Kissin' Cousins" With a Cow

The night was cold, fourteen degrees, but people were outside seated on the ground or on the hillside benches that overlooked a seven-acre cotton field across the public road. It was Christmastime.

Our local storekeeper and his wife had decided to use that seven acres each Christmas for the Lord. They asked our family to help them. Our friends placed lighted scenes of the life of Christ in the field. A giant twenty-four-foot-cross stood forty feet high on top of the tall hill behind the field. It beckoned to travelers for miles to come to the place where it shone. My husband did the narration, and music was inserted at the proper time. The sounds were amplified and could be heard by everyone. The scenes were individually lighted in sync with the unfolding of the story. On cold, crisp nights such as this one it was easy to feel a part of it all.

I don't know if it was by accident or part of the Lord's plan, but suddenly there was in our midst a huge cow. Mooing constantly. Running amuck among us. Scaring children, moms, dads, grandparents. Some few people rolled down the hills to get away. Those seated on benches overturned them in an effort to escape the rampaging animal. A few remained calm and tried to reassure others that all was well.

No one knew where the cow had come from or where she finally went. We never learned anything at all about her. We simply knew she was there and caused, not a cattle stampede, but a people one. We felt very much that we were like unhappy kissin' cousins to that cow. I think she was unhappy, too. She had become too much a part of us.

Some, who like to be able to explain everything, later said, " That's nothing to be upset about. The cow simply got out of her pasture, heard sounds, went toward them and became excited." A few wondered, "Do you suppose God sent that animal our way to make us realize that even the animals of the field are aware of Jesus' deity?" Others mockingly sang from the well known children's song, *The Farmer's in the Dell"*, "A moo, moo, here. A moo,moo, there. Here a moo, there a moo, everywhere a moo, moo." They passed off the incident lightly.

Years after the cow episode, I thought back to that Christmastime night. Everything had been still and wonderful. Then, suddenly, there was chaos. A few people panicked. Others assessed the situation and remained calm. Was there a lesson here for me? Was there coming a time when I would desperately need to be able to assess a situation and remain calm? Was this a behavior that God wanted me to learn? Was He leading me to a deeper understanding of some of the roles I would play in the future—roles that would require the kissin' cousins, a stout heart and a cool head, to be vital? The answer is, "Yes."

Kisses 'n More

A nineteen-year-old girl, strapped in a wheel chair, could neither move nor talk. Three or four years earlier she had been in a car accident and critically injured. One day I went to her home to see her. She was visibly excited. Her mother, even more so. The two of them had learned a way to communicate enough that the mother could anticipate her daughter's thoughts and needs. Because of this ability the mother was smiling and there was a hint of laughter in the girl's eyes. "Guess what," my hostess greeted me, "my daughter got a kiss today from a deer." Surely, I thought, I didn't hear what I think I did. "I'm sure he would like to give her another one," the mother continued, "and my daughter would love to have it."

My mind must be playing all sorts of tricks on her and on me, I thought. There is something going on here that I don't understand. I did not answer her at that moment.

Instead I reached over and patted the still hand of the young woman. Her mother left the room of their small mobile home while I greeted her daughter. When she returned she had with her, on a leash, a fawn—a baby white-tail deer.

Proudly the mother stroked the tiny head of the deer. "This baby likes to kiss my baby," she said. "They have so much in common." The little spotted one was straining at the leash, trying to reach the girl in the wheelchair.

My thoughts were still not all together. They were in a jumble, with unanswered questions. *What is this animal doing inside a house?* The law states that a wild animal cannot be kept as a pet without permission from proper authorities. *Where did she get him? How long has he been here? What does she feed him? What will happen to him when he grows up?* The questions came faster than answers could be supplied.

While I stood in that room, with my eyes still unbelieving, and my mind riding a questioning merry-go-round, the woman removed the leash. The little deer was free to go where he wished. He gave a tiny little yipping sound and bounced over to the wheelchair. The girl signaled her mother for help.

The baby animal had his front paws placed in a tiny open spot on the arm of the chair. The mother lifted her daughter's hand and placed it on the head of the little one who leaned over and "kissed" the injured girl. Then, very gently, he licked her face.

What a moment! It was as if God's presence was in that room directing a love scene. This was His kind of love— tender, careful and understanding— from one handicapped child to another. You see, the little fawn was orphaned when a car killed his mother, and he, himself, was blind.

The Winds of Music

A long time had passed since I had attended a Symphony Concert in the city. I missed the sounds of instruments being tuned, the subdued cacophony, the musicians dressed in formal blacks, and the elegance of the conductors. I sometimes longed to submerge my very being into lofty, blended sounds brought forth by instruments from the written scores of mighty composers. Being part of the setting for these concerts, albeit just as a member of the audience, was exhilarating and inspiring. I sometimes felt that God had to be near for such a wonder of awesome sounds to exist. I thought of composers such as Handel and Beethoven, and Liszt, who in later life became a priest and never charged a student for lessons. Much of their music was heartfelt praise to God.

I had lived apart from those experiences a long time, but I never forgot them. I thought of the woodwinds and their special sounds, the soothing voices of the strings, the blaring of the horns, and the astonishing sounds of the percussion section.

Since it was impossible for me to go to the city I began to look about me for substitutes. I became totally enamored of the Symphony of Sounds created by God, the Conductor. Looking back from the present, I see God's leadership not only of His Symphony Orchestra but also of my life.

Sitting alone on the front porch one evening, at just about the same time as a city concert would be tuning up, I began to hear things. There were peeper frogs resembling the sounds of fifes, and deep tuba voices of bullfrogs. Wind in the pines brought soothing notes played by a master violinist. There was the percussion sound of katydids in the trees, and the mighty solo voice of the great horned owl. The concert lasted for hours, and in the pre-dawn moments of the next day a woods thrush completed the concert with its soft, flute-like ending.

City and country had become as close as kissin' cousins. And God had been glorified.

WINSOME WEE ONES

Country Kids versus City Kids—and I Don't Mean Goats

Goats have kids and people have kids, but, one might say, 'They're certainly not the same kinds of kids."

Sometimes there is room for wondering about that. For example, take the matter of stubbornness. Goats are known for being "hard-headed". (There's no difference between city and country kids there). That doesn't mean simply that they have a hard, bony skull. It does mean they want to do what they want to do when they want to do it. Some human kids are the same way. Then, too, there are some children (kids) who behave as they do because of experiences they have had. (City kids may have more exposure to cultural things than country kids, but country kids have insights unknown to their counterparts). That may be good. Again, it may not.

Read on, and draw your own conclusions.

A Stubborn Little One Who Really Had a View

A precocious three-year-old girl from the city was visiting in the country. She and her parents had made a trip to an ocean side resort and stopped at a country Bed and Breakfast for the night on their return home. When her parents got up the next morning they couldn't find her. There was an outside entry to their room. The child was on the porch. Her mother called, "Come in, honey. You don't need to be out there alone."

"I don't want to come right now," the little girl said. "I want to stay right here." There was stubbornness to her tone. Her mother stepped outside, ready to punish her for disobedience. The child ran to her. "Oh, Mommy," she said, "I just couldn't come in yet." There was a look of wonder and awe on her face. She waved toward the farm pond that was close-by. "Isn't the ocean beautiful!"

Two Boys, Three Cats and a Tub of Water

Two five-year-old boys had been to the river one Sunday afternoon. There was a crowd of people there. And singing. And praying. And the preacher and three others stood in the middle of the waist deep river water. Our small community church was baptizing converts in the river, just as John the Baptist baptized Jesus in the River Jordan. There were very few country churches of that day that had inside baptistrys.

The two little fellows took it all in. One of the boys was the son of a deacon of the church; the other was ours. As soon as the baptismal service was completed, we were all to be together for an afternoon visit at the deacon's house.

His other children and ours were playing in the yard. The bright sun and humidity flushed their little faces as if they were bitten by blasts of icy wind. But there was no wind, and there was no ice. On the porch, the adults sat in rocking chairs and stirred the air with cardboard fans furnished by the local funeral home. We were talking of such things as crops and lack of rain and planning for the continuation of the stirring of the Holy Spirit that resulted from the revival meeting. We looked out into the yard when, suddenly, we were aware that there was silence—no children's laughter (or quarreling), no games of Hide and Seek or Pitch Ball. Just stillness.

"Wonder where the kids went?" I asked the deacon's wife.

"I'm sure they're O.K.," she said, "probably just around at the back of the house. They may have gone to cool off at the water pump."

"Let's see if we can find them," I suggested. Before we could get to the back of the house, one of the children screamed, then ran toward us. "Mama, Mama," she cried to my hostess. "They're drowning the kittens!"

We took the tiny girl by the hand and ran as fast as we could. "Whatever would cause anyone to drown the kittens?" my friend panted.

We came to an abrupt halt when we heard the voices of two little boys. They both were crying. "What happened, Son," I asked mine. The other child was hiding behind his mother. She was trying to console him. A zinc tub of water was under the water pump.

Her little fellow answered the question I had asked. "We were having a baptizing. There were three kittens just like there were people at the river this afternoon. We wanted them to go to heaven when they died and we thought they should be baptized, too." His little body shook with sobs. Then he looked at me. "I was the song leader," he said. "We sang 'Shall We Gather at the River' and 'On Jordan's Stormy Banks'. We didn't know all the words, but we remembered some of them from this afternoon. Then pointing to our son, "He was the preacher. He was doing the baptizing just like his daddy. We had a prayer and after that he said, 'I now baptize you in the name of the Father, the Son, and the Holy Ghost.'"

At this point my little son began to cry loudly. "Mom," he said, "I was trying to baptize him and he wiggled, and when I finally got him to be still under the water I took him out." He burst into hard sobs. "Look at him, Mom. He won't move. Did I kill him?" The child shook the bedraggled kitten gently. "I was just trying to help him."

The kitten was dead—drowned. And my son felt like a murderer rather than a true servant of the Lord. He had tried to follow the pattern set by Jesus that he had heard his daddy preach about, but he did not understand the true meaning of it all, and everything went wrong.

I cried with the children. We buried the baby cat. We had a funeral service.

We all learned something that hot, sultry, summer day:

We must not do something just because we watched someone else do that thing. We must know the true, real reasons for our actions.

As a parent and a Christian I had to acknowledge my faulty part in this. I had thought my son was too young to understand. He wasn't, but he did need correct understanding.

Don't we all? Just a smattering of the truth won't suffice.

On another occasion this same son and his siblings were at home with their grandparents. My husband was to give the eulogy at a funeral. I was with him. As we drove in from the service we noticed all three of the kids had somber faces. We stopped the car beside a hole they had dug.

"What's up?" my husband asked.

"We're having a funeral service," our small daughter said. Then she grinned. "But there's nothing in the box. We're just pretending."

"We did sing a song," the boys chimed in.

"What was its name?" I asked.

At this point they all sang the old spiritual, "Ev'rybody Talkin' 'Bout Heav'n Ain't Goin' There".

Do Trees Talk?

After having lived in the country for a number of years I was much more relaxed and "educated" than I had been earlier. In fact, there was a feeling of camaraderie when I walked in the forest that surrounds the house. Most of the time we did our walking as a family. The children ran and jumped over logs and in quiet moments watched for squirrels that might be playing "Catch me, if you can".

One day, after such an excursion, our three-year-old son said, "Mom, I'm going outside for a little while." He often enjoyed playing in his own way. I went about my usual work, keeping a casual eye on him as I did so. Then I missed him. He had moved from his regular play spot. Quickly I went to the back door to check the yard there.

He was climbing up to the top of the picnic table. There he stood. Then, with his sweet, piping voice he began to sing praises to God for the trees, the animals of the woods, and even the ground puppies (black with white spots salamanders) that we sometimes used as bait to catch catfish. He sang for perhaps fifteen minutes. His praise concert ended with a return to his praise for the trees. Somehow, their majesty spoke to him of the majesty of the Creator. He safely exited his "stage" and resumed his play in the front yard.

That same evening our little daughter took the hand of her grandmother. "Let's sit on the back steps," she begged. As they sat there, the moon gave enough light to chase away a little of the darkness. They quietly embraced the night beauty and its sounds. Not talking. Not moving. Simply immersing themselves in the awesome presence of God's creations. Just before time to go inside, our three-year-old daughter, twin to the tabletop singer, looked at her grandmother and said the only words of their time together. "Aren't the 'twees bootiful?"

Did the trees talk? Not out loud, but they spoke through

their very being to our twins. God is so gracious in His blessings to us.

"I Will Not Say I'm Sorry"

Our son was five years old, with a mind of his own. He had disobeyed and needed to be aware that there were consequences. "You know you did what you were told not to do, don't you?" I asked. Then I continued, "Tell Mommy you are sorry."

He refused.

Again, I insisted he say, "I'm sorry".

Silence.

"Son, if you don't tell me you are sorry, I will have to punish you. Get me a little switch."

My small boy opened the door and went out. But he didn't come back. I began to look for him. He was rounding the curve in our private drive that leads to the public road. Many thoughts crossed my mind. Is he running away from home? Surely he's not that upset. Was I too harsh? Did he hate me and want nothing to do with me? What should I do?

His small hands were clasped behind him, his head bowed, his shoulders were drooping as he went out of sight.

In a big hurry to reach him before he got to the public road, I ran as fast as I could. When I got to the place where I could see him, he was no longer walking on our drive but had stepped over into the side ditch. I waited, out of sight, until I saw him turn toward the house. I quickly retraced my steps and was waiting at the door when he finally trudged toward the house. His hands still were clasped behind him. His head was lowered, but his shoulders were squared back. They gave the only sign of determination.

I stepped out on the porch to meet him. "Where have you been, Son?" I asked. He did not answer. "Are you ready to tell me you are sorry for doing wrong?"

He stopped when he was very close to me. How I wanted to reach out and take him into my arms and cry with him, but I thought he needed discipline first. Looking up at me I saw tears flowing from his eyes, but the words "I am sorry" were not uttered. Instead, he unclasped his hands from behind him, and gestured toward me. In that tiny hand which he held out to me was a bouquet of wild flowers. His offering of sorrow. Sorrow because he could not do what I asked.

God really convicted me that day. I had tried to *make* my son tell a lie. There was no sorrow in his heart. He had done nothing wrong. I later found out I was the one at fault. The child had not disobeyed.

My son loved me enough to forgive me! It was I who needed to say to him and to my Heavenly Father, "I'm sorry."

DOES GOD HAVE A
FUNNY BONE?

Rainy Day Blues

In accepting God's plan for my life He taught me many things; among them that He has a sense of humor. His wit makes the necessary stresses of life a little lighter and the smiles on faces a lot brighter. He has taught me that life is not always sad, troubled, unhappy, unpleasant. He wants His children to be joyful, even playful. He also wants us to partake of some R. & R. (rest and relaxation).

The day had begun as it had twenty-nine of the thirty days of that June. The sky was weeping rain again. The trees wore lush foliage and the flowers flourished because of those tears. "Not another rainy day," I muttered, then said in a complaining voice to God, "When will it stop?"

God and I often carry on conversations where I, like Job of old, ask questions of Him. He doesn't answer audibly, but He directs my thoughts to His answer. That is what He did this time.

I became aware of His answering. "Do you see?" came the explanation. "I have a plan for the betterment of my people. You may not understand, but knowing that I do should be sufficient."

"But, Father," I said, "I'm so tired of no sunshine."

I moved to a window, preparing to moan again about the rain, but what I saw was a bright sunray peeping through the sky spaces between the tree leaves. I moved to another window. The sun smiled at me there. At the third window facing eastward I glimpsed the full brightness of the morning sun. It lingered for only a second, and was gone. The rain continued, but my mood was now upbeat and cheerful. God had played "Peep-eye" with me, and that made my day.

Does God Answer Stupid Prayers?

I have to say that He does, because He has answered some of mine.

I was standing in water almost over the top of my hip boots. For several days rain had been constant. The waters of a large lake had risen and spilled out and flooded a huge area of land. I had gone there to fish. On one side were small bushes inundated by the flood; on the other, dead limbs and brush brought along with the rapid rise of the lake. A camera hung around my neck. There was always one there when I was out in God's world of nature.

I looked to my left. A couple of harmless water snakes were swimming around. The same picture was on my right. They seemed to be enjoying their new scenery outside the confines of the lake. I knew they were harmless. I dismissed their presence. A friend was seated on the limb of a tree that had the floodwaters at its feet. I glanced toward him. He held up a string of huge crappie that he had caught.

As I looked away from him I saw, about seventy-five feet in front of me the largest cottonmouth moccasin I had ever seen. In its mouth was a channel catfish that probably weighed two pounds.

It is a virtual impossibility to run in hip-deep water. My

best action would be to remain still. Then I had a bright idea. I remembered the camera around my neck. What a great picture that snake with its fish would make! Hastily, I prayed. "Lord, please let that snake come close enough for me to get a good picture, but don't let him come too close."

I watched in awe as that poisonous reptile, still holding the fish, turned and swam straight toward me. Then I snapped to attention as it came within good camera range. I took the picture. Immediately, the snake did a U-turn and swam away. I saw him no more.

Many times I wondered what God must have thought of me for bothering Him with that stupid prayer. I also wondered why He answered it.

I learned the who, when, what and why about the incident one day. I had been asked to be Keynote Speaker at a Women's Conference, on the subject of Missions. Just before my time on the program the person in charge came to me. "I've done a terrible thing," she said. "I've been so busy trying to put this conference together that I failed to tell you we want you to speak on Prayer instead of on Missions." She apologized profusely. Then, in her embarrassing predicament she asked, "Is there *any way* you can change?"

Five minutes is not much time to work up a Keynote speech, but God, being *(who)* He is, knew there would come a time *(when)* I would need His help again. This was it. *(What)* I would say would be prefaced by the story of the prayer and the snake.

The answer to *(why)* He honored that petition became crystal clear. He wanted these women to be assured that He hears and pays attention, and probably smiles, at even our most stupid and foolish requests.

Duck!

There is so much to learn about God just by observing

what surrounds us. In my days of acceptance of God's placement of me in the country I began to see all kinds of glimpses of God's caring, not only for Man but also for other things. He provides for their needs.

One beautiful October day I was standing near a large tree on the riverbank. I heard a whir of wings, slipped behind the tree and peeped out. A flock of mallard ducks settled onto the water just in front of me. They seemed restless. I knew they had not spotted me, so I wasn't the cause of their unrest. A few minutes passed before a large mallard drake swam toward the riverbank, scuttled up the short distance from the water to the ground and began to walk upstream.

From my special viewpoint behind the tree I watched and listened. He gave a single "quack". Ducks began to follow him. Soon the river was empty of them. They were standing, single file, right behind him.

A large tree, probably pushed over by strong winds, lay two-thirds of the distance across the river. Only the tree trunk remained. The limbs and leaves had long ago floated downstream. The lead duck hopped upon the log that was anchored several feet on the shore. Without a backward glance he began walking. The line of perhaps twenty ducks followed about a foot apart.

At the end of the log the first duck paused. When he did, the second duck sneaked up behind him and pushed him off into the water. While that was taking place the third duck pushed the second one off the log. This continued until each duck had been shoved into the river. Immediately, the lead duck led the others into playing their game again. This time there was much fluttering of wings, and quacking that sounded as if they were giggling at each other.

When the last duck stood alone at the end of their tree trunk bridge, he leaped high, flapped his wings, and dropped into the water. At that instance, a peculiar thing happened. The ducks dispersed. Each swam to a secluded spot under the overhang of the shoreline, put head beneath wing, and went to sleep.

What an insight! God had allowed me a view of His perfect plan of rest and relaxation. Those ducks, unlike so many of us humans, were wise enough to rid themselves of the stress of their long flight with a time of relaxation and rest.

I had so much fun watching those ducks. I wonder if God took off a moment from His eternal plans and laughed at "duck antics", too.

Baskets and Angels, Bells and Owls

I believe God enjoys answering our prayers, even the inconsequential ones. Furthermore I believe He has a good time answering them in an abundant manner. In my case I once needed a really nice, fancy basket. I didn't even have an unfancy one. Following a pattern of many years, I prayed. This was a simple prayer, "Father, I understand this is not a need of great consequence but, please, may I somehow be able to own a nice basket?"

Guess what! I received a basket, as a gift. Not only was it ideal for my purpose, but it was filled with fruit. God is so abundantly gracious. He had taken time from His duties of the Universe to listen and to reply graciously.

Not only did I receive that basket, but within a short period my basket collection was so large that I could have done as a neighbor did and used them to make a truly unusual décor statement. The reason I didn't is that I didn't want to be a copycat even though I admired her basket room greatly.

At an after-Christmas sale several years ago I bought two Christmas angels. Over the years I have been supplied with angels of many descriptions. No two are alike. I have not bought one since those first two. They have all been gifts. I enjoy them immensely. I do not worship angels. I do not talk to these angels. I do appreciate the loveliness of the handmade ones.

I did not ask God for any of these angels as I had for that first basket. He had already supplied me with a real one. The Scriptures tell us He sends His guardian angels to watch over us. Perhaps my friends, the gift givers, were simply reminding me of God's care for me. I wonder anew, does God smile at my over-abundance?

Then there is the subject of bells. I think God understands my propensity for collecting things. There are bells from everywhere; reminders of places I have been, of church bells hanging in tall steeples, waiting to call worshipers to gather.

One of the bells is in the form of a little Dutch girl carrying water. Water is a symbol of Holland. It is also a symbol of Who Jesus is. He said, in John 4:10 to the woman at the well of whom he had asked a drink of water, "If you knewest the gift of God, and who it is that saith to thee, Give me a drink; thou wouldest have asked of him, and he would have given thee living water."

Owls have fascinated me since I met a man who could make a sound so like a great horned owl that even the real bird wouldn't know the difference. Like the bird he mimics he had a lot of spunk and ingenuity.

Once he was in the hospital, and had been given a sedative. The effect of the medicine began to lessen, and the man became confused. He was aware of bright lights and thought the hospital was on fire. He tried to summons a nurse, but none came.

Finally, in desperation, he did the only thing he could think of to get help. He loudly gave the call of the great horned owl. The hooting sound that was so familiar to him, but not to the hospital staff, brought doctors and nurses running down the hall to his room.

Since that time I have been an admirer of owls. I let this

be known once, and now I have a wonderful collection of owls. Aren't friends wonderful? And to think, God gave me a special collection of friends, too.

God really must have a funny bone. When baskets, angels, bells, owls and friends all are all heaped together in one life, surely He grins at the concoction.

Three Snooky-Snakes

Much as I dislike snakes, God has used them, with humor, to teach me to trust Him. He sent a prime example of this one June morning. For one of our magazine articles we needed a picture of a snake. We had not seen one of those slithering creatures all year long. So, I did what I felt was necessary, and prayed. I must have prayed, believing, for I had a camera in my hand and was already at the door leading outside the house. Before I stepped out our little fice dog began to bark.

Yes. There was God's answer to my prayer. A non-poisonous "spreading adder". That is what this particular kind of reptile (Hog-Nose snake) is called in our area. He is frightening to look at. When upset, his normally long narrow head spreads out into the shape of the vicious, poisonous asp. Spreading adders must have pleased God. The appearance of this "lesser" creature causes God's final creation, Man, to back off. That is one way of looking at how God warns us of possible sins. He causes us to stop, look, and listen before we venture forth; to think before we move into harm's way.

I snapped the picture. Even as I did so, I heard the dog bark again. I went to him. There was another spreading adder. It had climbed into a small bush. As I pressed the camera shutter, that little dog had located a third snake of the same kind.

Now God knew I only needed one snake picture. I like

to think He was playfully showing me His power. I hope His pleasure from my astonishment at His provision was as great as the thankfulness I felt from His three-fold answer to a non-vital prayer.

GOD

Walking and Talking

God and I walked in the woods today. I could see His handprints, His footprints. The beauty He created must have brought a gleam of pleasure to His eyes.

A light mist was falling. The tree leaves appeared with shining tears as if grateful that God took time out to review His creations, and to be a part of their lives.

Remembrances of other walks with Him came to mind. We had walked together in good times, sad times, funny times. He had taken my hand and led me through the deep forests of Life. He had been, and is, my Comforter, Counselor, King and Saviour. On this day we were walking as Mentor and student, companions and friends. Memories were almost overwhelming.

We passed the tree with the pool of spring water at its base. One of the roots bent out about halfway across the pool, then made a U-turn back to the foot of the parent tree. Often I thought of the lesson of that tree root. It adventured on its own. How often I have done that. It seemed to have become afraid. I've had a battle with that emotion a number of times. It returned to the safety of its parent tree.

There, at that spot, I thanked God for being my
Heavenly Father, for the security and comfort of His love,
for His leadership and guidance through the years.

As we continued our walk, other memories surfaced.

The Anniversary Tree

A lone pine stands on a large, rounded mound of earth.
Its roots are firmly set into deep fertile soil. Its thick trunk
supports a crown of twisted limbs that seem always to be
reaching heavenward. It was to this tree my husband and I
took our last walk together. We had gone there many times
before. It had been a type of altar at which we recommitted
ourselves anew to God and to each other. Very shortly after
this walk his mode of movement was a wheelchair.

As God and I paused at the Anniversary Tree, I shed
tears of joy and thanksgiving to Him for the blessing of the
good and faithful leadership He had given us, and the
adventures in following Him that brought so much happiness and peace.

Typewriters and Doodle Bug Races

God and I walked to Hickory Nut Hill. This was always
a favorite family spot. We visited there in every season. In
fall the squirrels and we gathered the sweet hickory nuts that
were the fruit of the trees. In winter, we flushed rabbits from
the underbrush where they hid. In spring we reveled in
beautiful wildflowers that poked heads from beneath the
autumn's covering of leaves. In summer we often piled kids,
typewriters, and stove wood blocks, to be used as desks and
seats, into the car and headed for the hill. There we set up
our typewriters and worked on manuscripts while the children ran and roamed and played freely. One memorable day
our little daughter came running to us. Excitement showed

in her face. "Look," she said. "I've found a beetle-bug. It's so neat and shiny black." She showed her treasure to us.

"That's a Betsy-bug, Honey," my husband said. I left my stove-wood-block- typewriter-chair and went for a view of the bug. I had never seen one. My husband looked at me and grinned. "Did you know this little bug could show you where the cows are?"

By this time the other children had gathered around and together they all said, "Aw, Daddy, you know better than that!"

"I learned that fact as a small boy when my parents sent me into the big pasture to bring home the cows," he continued. "Sometimes I didn't know where they were. Then I learned to look for Betsy-bugs. The saying goes that if you find a Betsy-bug tell it, 'Show me where the cows are.' The bug will take off in their direction."

Our daughter stood with one hand on a hip, the bug in the other. She had been taught to believe in the truth of what her father said, but this was more than she could go along with. "Put the bug on the ground," he told her. "Now say the magic words."

She did. Nothing happened. "I knew this bug didn't know about cows," she said.

"Oh, but maybe he does," my husband countered. "He's not moving, so he must understand that we have no cows."

Still unconvinced about the cow thing, our daughter asked, "What does this bug really do?"

"Really and truly," her dad answered, "when I was your age your uncle and I often found a little place of cleared ground and, using small sticks as posts and winding string around them, built a fence. Inside our 'pasture' we kept Betsy-bug 'horses'. We had races with our bug horses. We harnessed them with string to little match box 'wagons' and had a race to see which would win."

There was an immediate search by the children for more

Betsy-bugs. Typewriters and deadlines were of no importance for a little while. We all played Betsy-bug games, then turned the bugs loose. They were not harmed, and we were relaxed and happy.

The Trail of Tears

I spoke to my Lord one day as we walked. "Lord," I said, "I can't walk this trail. There are too many memories." And He just kept urging me along. We passed the place where our children used to hunt for ground puppies (black with white dotted salamanders used as fish bait for catfish). The kids always vied with each other to see who could find the most. The winner was allowed to set out the first fishing hook, and to have first choice of where to place it. Always there was hope that the biggest fish would be snagged on the hook.

As we traveled favored paths, I realized one of the prime reasons for our walk was that I might have renewed hope and stronger faith, accompanied by joy. God's adventures are always for a reason. On this particular day my emotions were bound up in tears and an empty heart. They also were encompassed with thanksgiving and a look toward the future. I suppose you could use the oxymoron "a light, heavy heart". How can anyone have a light heart that is heavy at the same time? There are ways. A light heart might be one that is joyful and hopeful. A heavy one could be filled with sorrow and woe. But when God is in command He orders a diet of joy and hope for believers even as they partake of unspeakable agonies.

I repeated, "Lord, I don't think I can walk this way today." Looking behind me there was emptiness. A void. Almost a vacuum. We had walked this trail together as a family many times. Now I was alone.

Our oldest son had died a few weeks earlier. He and his younger brother had been in the hospital at the same time, in rooms across the hall from each other. At first we were told of the probability that neither of the boys would live. The older boy had Meningitis; the younger, Acute Rheumatic Fever. Our daughter was shifted from neighbor's house to neighbor's house while her father and I were at the hospital. He came home each night, picked her up, even if she were already asleep, and carried her to the house. They had breakfast together. She then went to school; he, to the hospital. The heart crush of being away from her was acute and chronic pain.

After several weeks at the hospital we were told there was a chance our youngest son would live, but there was no hope for our older son. In those last weeks before his death, I was informed by the doctors that we could not go from one child's room to the other. There was too much danger of the transfer of infections. We had to choose which child needed us most. We could open the door to the other's room and look in, but could not enter it. There was no way to hold that child's hand or give him a hug. Saying from afar, "I love you," was all I could do. Sorrow, sadness, anxiety and the aching longing to be with both boys and our daughter was almost beyond bearing.

Now, as I walked this trail, our two younger children were at home with their father. Our son was recovering, but he would be an invalid for at least six more months. Our daughter went off to school each morning, bravely trudging through each day, fearful that she would find us gone again when she got home. My husband and the children all had urged me to get away from the house for a little while. I used the opportunity for these quiet moments with the Lord to strengthen my faith, to cry out to Him and to find the comfort and courage I so desperately needed.

"Oh, Lord," I protested, "this is too hard. Not only is there death to deal with, but the children, now at home, still have feelings of neglect and—yes—favoritism." I sat beneath a great white oak, and continued my outpouring to God. "They were too young, Lord, to understand the choices that had to be made— to stay with them or be with their brother as he died." I stood up. God and I continued our walk in silence. To me, the trail was desolate and despairing.

It is not in God's heart to leave us with those feelings. He comforted me with His Word. His Presence was with me. His love overwhelmed me. My heart became lighter because of His leading me beside still waters. The heaviness was easier to bear because He said in His Word, "...I will never leave thee nor forsake thee" (Hebrews 13:5). He hasn't.

Amblin' Ramblin'

God and I continued to walk and commune. One day several years later our stroll took us to the banks of Autry Creek; the same little Creek, the same spot where I had been so frightened and fearful of all the trees around me. This was the exact place I had learned to identify forty kinds of tree leaves so that I could be at ease in the land I now claim as home.

To get to this spot we had walked deer paths, pushed our way through briar thickets and jumped over fallen logs. I had learned to greet each day as a new adventure, each hour a joy, and each moment a time for thanksgiving. With only His kind of love and His kind of patience had I made it to this point.

As we stood by the singing waters of the stream I could hear beyond its song the sounds of cars traveling on paved roads. I realized God had brought me full circle back to my beginnings of true service to Him. I now had a choice. The children were grown and had their own families. My husband had died, and I was free to go back to the city. I knew my answer just a few days before his death.

I was sitting beside his bed. We were holding hands. He

didn't talk much now, but he looked at me and said, "When I'm gone, what will you do? Will you move back to the city?" I didn't even have to think about it. I knew the answer.

"No, I said, "this will always be my home until we meet again in heaven."

He closed his eyes and slept peacefully.

On the banks of our little creek, on this day of ambling and rambling with God, I found peace also. My journey with Him had ended for the day, but a new day would dawn, a new adventure would be mine. It did not matter where in this world that might take place.

I had been in the country for forty years. God, the Potter, had been molding me and making me, shaping me and breaking me. The time was near for what I had become, through His hands-on adventures, to move toward the work that waited.

In His graciousness, God has prepared me for, and placed me in, situations far beyond anything taught in schools of higher learning. When He is the professor, that's the ultimate. I do not yet have a Master or Doctorate degree from His University of City-Country Ways and Means, but He is still the greatest teacher in heaven and earth.

Soon after my husband's death I again felt God's moving in my life. As a city-bred fourteen year old Christian I had committed my life to be an emissary, a missionary wherever He led. Ten years later His Tour of Duty led to rural areas where it lasted four decades. Now, the path began to curve, back and forth, back and forth in almost dizzying turns.

Remembrances of that long ago teenage promise surfaced. I called our denomination's Missions office. I needed information, thinking of some form of volunteer work in one of the nearby states in our country. When I first said the words "volunteer missions", his response was: "I've been waiting for you. I knew you would call."

"How can that be?" I questioned. "I didn't know even an hour ago I would be wanting information. I don't even know your name."

"No, but God does, and He knows yours, too. We need one more lady to complete a group who will be teaching children in Argentina. We'll be leaving in three weeks. I'll be talking with you several times before then."

I had to sit down. In five minutes, through God's leadership, I had moved from a quiet, peaceful—although sometimes lonely—life to a period of new challenges and new adventures with the Lord.

FLYING ISN'T JUST FOR THE BIRDS

It's For All of God's Children

My stepson called. He was once an Air Force pilot. Now he is a *frequent* (meaning a lot of the time) flyer. He goes everywhere. He knew I had not flown in at least forty years. Actually, I had never flown. As a college senior I once boarded a plane with seven other senior girls to be in an advertisement for an airline. That was IT.

"I want to help you," he told me, "not to be afraid to fly."

I needed that. Fear had sometimes plagued me in my country life. In this new phase, I wanted no part of it. I berated myself. Would I never learn to trust God with everything?

Even in my weakness God was showing his strength. Help for me was lovingly provided. By the time my son finished mentoring me on the ways of airplanes, my fears left and I was "flying high" with excitement. My bags were packed. Camera equipment for the photojournalism I was to do was in top-notch condition. Lesson materials and gifts for the children I would work with were in separate luggage. My companions and I took off for Buenos Aires, six thousand miles away. There were five of us, eleven pieces of luggage and my camera bag.

A woman, driving a small car, met us at Ezeiza Airport. She hired two independent cabs and we headed for the Mission Compound. The cab drivers parked on the sidewalk in front of Mission Headquarters and unloaded the luggage. My camera bag was missing. The cabs bore no identification, the driver's names were not known. It seemed this trip had already suffered defeat in the photojournalism area.

"Where are You, Lord?" I questioned. "I followed You here. Now a large part of my reason for being here is a failure before I ever start." I went out to the sidewalk again. The bag still wasn't there.

Inside, my four friends had begun to pray. The time was about noon. None of us was hungry. We simply wanted to locate that bag and get on with our purpose. Following God is not always easy. We do not understand His ways. Their prayers were not answered.

At three o'clock my friends decided to pray again. This time they would be more specific. "Father," they prayed, "we know You have a blessing waiting for us concerning this camera bag. You know why it is needed. You know where it is. We humbly pray that You will cause something to happen to cause the cab driver to look in the trunk of his car, see Lola's bag, and bring it back."

At six o'clock there was a knock at the door. The cab driver stood there, speaking rapidly in Spanish. He said, "At three o'clock this afternoon, (the exact time of the second prayer) I smelled smoke in my car. I looked, and it was coming from the back. I opened the trunk. My cab was on fire. Two bare wires were crossed and had caused it. I saw this bag."

The driver looked directly at me and said, "I disconnected the wires, then grabbed your bag. I'm bringing it back to you." Then he folded his hands as a child does in the posture of prayer and said, "Isn't God good!"

God had given to each of us an adventure in relying on His power and His sovereignty and His love in yet another way.

Flying by the Seat of Your Pants

I did that once.

In China.

On a remodeled Chinese Air Force plane, turned passenger friendly—almost.

I was with a group of tourists, but three of us in the group were having an adventure with God. We were seeking to learn all we could about the amount of freedom of worship of Christ in that several billion-population country. We had some Bibles with us. Taking a few Bibles into the country was not really illegal, but could have caused problems. God had graciously arranged that our luggage not be inspected from the time we left home until we were back in the states. We wanted to leave those Mandarin Chinese Bibles with people who were Christians and could use them.

We boarded the plane. There were no assigned seats. No flight attendants, per se. There were a couple of women who seemed to be in charge, but for the most part they stayed in the forward compartment. No announcements about oxygen masks and flotation gear. No checking of seat belts, seats back and trays up.

Without warning, the plane took off in an almost straight up flight. About a third of the passengers with aisle seats were standing up when the pilot made the sudden ascent. Some of us didn't rise with it. Instead we were flying backwards by the seat of our pants before we landed in the aisle floor or in someone's lap. No one was hurt, and we all laughed at the spectacle, but there was no standing up the rest of the flight, and the descent was as fast and unexpected as the take-off had been.

I wondered if my flight to heaven would be this sudden and this fast? What an adventure that will be!

Egypt, Japan, With Oragami in the Middle

The plane was crowded. The passenger list would have fit any international aggregate. My seatmate was a young woman from Japan. In her left hand she held a package of small, square pieces of colored paper. In her right hand she held a single piece that she had folded several times. I glanced at her and smiled. She said, in English, "Would you like to have this?"

She handed me a beautifully formed peacock made of one of the little squares. Ah—I thought, Oragami, the art of designing objects simply by knowing how to fold paper—a Japanese art form. I knew, at that moment, that God was handing me an opportunity for an adventure.

We talked. She told of her education and her view of life. The last gave me an opportunity to ask of her religion.

"Religion?" she asked. "I have none."

"Then, may I tell you about Jesus, and what He has done for you?"

She nodded assent, but said, "Who is Jesus? I've never heard of Him."

What a shock! In my secluded little country spot everyone had heard of Jesus. They might not know him personally, but they knew of Him. This was my very first experience with someone who had never heard of Christ.

The Jesus story can become complicated if you try to tell it in anyway but the simplest to one who knows nothing of it. "What am I to do, Lord?" I silently prayed. " I don't know how to begin. I don't know how to tell about You to someone who has never heard of You."

I tried to make her understand, but this blessed truth, to

the young woman beside me, seemed totally a made-up story. Finally, I asked if she would like me to send her a Bible when I got back home. She said, "Yes." I sent her a small English language Gideon New Testament. Where I live, Japanese New Testaments are not easily procured. I knew she spoke English, and I was in a hurry for her to read about Jesus and His love.

A few weeks later I received a letter from her. She wrote: "I've tried to understand the little Book you sent, but I get all mixed up because I don't know all the words in English. Could you send me a copy written in Japanese?" Through the International Bible Society I found one and sent it to her. We corresponded for several years, but she never mentioned Jesus.

Ten years later I was in Japan. We planned to meet in Tokyo. As she entered the hotel room she carried a shopping bag. In it she had a gift for me. I had one for her. After exchanging those, she took a small black box from the bag. Carrying it in both hands as if it were very precious she brought it to me. Carefully she opened the box. In it, softly cushioned, lay the Japanese New Testament I had sent her.

Tearfully, she said, "But I still don't understand it."

How difficult it is to show God's way to one who is totally ignorant of Who He is. I tried to explain the Plan of Salvation as simply as possible. .

We hugged as she left, shed tears, and hugged again— and she was gone. For a few years we kept in touch. I read in the newspaper about an earthquake where she lived. There was much loss of life. I sent her a letter. It was returned, and I have not heard from her since the earthquake. I can only pray that understanding of God's plan and surrender to Him did take place.

I'll Fly Away

I don't expect my flight to be on the wings of a snow-white dove, as in the song a country singer often performed. I don't know how the residents at the nursing home, where I teach a weekly Bible Study, feel about the method God will use for transportation to heaven. I do know that the Bible speaks of the angels carrying Lazarus into Abraham's bosom. I presume they flew. What I am sure of is that the people who attend the Bible Study thoroughly enjoy singing that "old-timey" song, *I'll Fly Away*. They like the up-beat movement of the music and the imagery of flying surrounded by angels. Sometimes it seems they equate their "home-going" with that of Lazarus.

One day, at the close of our study a lady raised her hand and asked, "Could we sing my favorite song?"

Several others joined in her plea. As I played the introduction, one of the residents began to move her arms up and down like wings. Soon everyone was laughing and singing and flapping away.

That day, as I started to leave, instead of hearing "good-byes" from the group I heard the noise of flapping "wings". I flapped back. We ended that session with a smile on every face.

PO' FOLKS' HOUSES, KINGS' PALACES, AND MCDONALD'S ON EVERY CORNER

Dirt Floors, Mud Ovens, Smiles and Hugs

Many years after I cooked all our meals in the fireplace, learned the art of using wood-burning cook stoves, and finally reverted to my city know-how in operating an electric stove, I was in Honduras on a Mission trip. High up in the mountains I met a lady who lived in the country. Through the help of a woman from the United States she began baking loaves of white bread such as we buy here. This type bread was new to her village. She became so adept at her new trade that she created a great reputation and made a good living for her family. I was to write about experiences in Honduras, so I visited her home where she did the baking.

My missionary friend who knew the way to the house drove along a small gravel road to a gate in a pasture fence. I got out and unhooked the barbed wire that curled around the gatepost as a fastener. After she drove through I retied the wire and we drove down a dirt lane toward the house.

On our left were goats mulling around a small shack. Just beyond were fresh-washed clothes hanging on a line. We rounded a bend in the road, and parked in the yard in front of the house. The house was set on a small rise. It was square-built, and had at one time worn a coat of paint. Now the weathered gray of its wooden boards had only a few proud streaks of dirty white.

Waiting for us at the door was a wonderful lady with a beautiful smile and a warm welcome. Her husband and children stood nearby. We stepped inside onto a smooth, dust free, dirt floor. Oil from bare feet had made the earthen floor slick and shiny. On the floor, to the left of the chair in which I sat, lay a doll forgotten by its little owner in the excitement of having visitors. The house was divided into several rooms through the use of curtains and hanging quilts. I did not notice any inside doors. On a table to my right were loaves of homemade bread. Hanging on the wall above the bread was an original painting done by the oldest son. The husband excused himself to return to his part of the family business. His job was to bag and seal the loaves.

"Would you like to see my stoves?" our hostess asked.

"Stoves?" I questioned.

"Yes. In fact, I have three, and they're all different." First she led me to her electric stove. I could see how proud she was of it. Having this stove was one of the results of her bread baking business.

She led me to the second stove. It was black cast-iron, and wood burning. The chrome on it was rubbed to a high gleam, and the cast-iron was as polished as a new pair of black patent-leather shoes. Then she said, "My other stove is outside."

To the right of the doorsteps as we went into the yard stood a baked mud stove, hard as a brick, and inside the open oven the temperature was perfect for baking. "This is my best oven," she said. "Bread in it always come out right."

Suddenly my thoughts turned to the baking of bread in the city. For a moment I forgot my country learning, and reverted to my city upbringing. Surely, the electric stove, or even the wood stove, was better. She had just not yet realized their convenience.

Then I returned to the reality that country people often have come up with their own ways of dealing with circumstances. Some of their solutions are so simple as to be overlooked in the grand, ever-searching for the more elaborate, more expensive, shinier and newer products. This brilliant woman and others have used what was available to them and made what was needed, even though there might not have been even a penny to spend on that need. That is what she did when she made the mud stove. Sometimes things we make, using our own creativity, have more meaning to us than anything we buy.

I remembered, from years before, my makeshift oven in our fireplace and how, after I mastered the art of cooking that way, food tasted better than I ever thought possible.

I was intrigued with the stove. She had told me how she shaped it of mud and let it dry in the sun, but I still had questions. "How do you heat it to just the right temperature?" I asked.

She laughed. "Practice. I burned the crust of several loaves before I learned how many sticks of wood to put into the firebox."

"What about the children playing?"

"They're not allowed in the front yard when the oven is hot." Then she added the answer to one more question— What makes this stove better than the other two for baking the loaves?

. I was expecting her to say, "I don't know. It just does." But she had the answer. "The reason the mud stove bakes better than the other stoves is that it stays at the same temperature without cooling off and then having to re-heat to the correct temperature. Somehow that gives the bread a different flavor to those baked in other kinds of ovens. Besides, in summer time it doesn't make the house hot. In winter, we don't need it for heat."

I could talk her language. I had been there.

We went back into the house to say our good-byes to the entire family. The little ones gave me a sweet childish hug and held onto my hands as we went out the door. The husband gave us a gift of freshly baked and packaged bread and his wife smiled and thanked us for coming.

What a gentle and genteel time we had in that old house that lacked many of the so-called necessities for living, but actually was filled with the true necessities of life—Jesus Christ, and the attributes that distinguish those who follow His way—faith, hope, and love.

City—country—it didn't matter. I thanked God for a smattering of knowledge of both. I found that time spent in both places helped me to fit in wherever I was.

Palaces, Fishing Boats and City Ways

Fitting in applies equally to circumstances. I was in Cairo, Egypt. The Omar Khayyam palace, named for the great poet, was built in 1869 to celebrate the opening of the Suez Canal. It rests on the island of Gezira in the middle of the Nile River. The opera Aida composed by Guiseppe Verdi was first performed in this palace, and Empress Eugenie, wife of Napoleon, was invited to spend time here. This palace, now known as the Cairo Marriott Hotel, was my place of residence while I was there.

Outside, the building shone like gold. Inside, there was luxury and beauty, and the feel of the presence of royalty was almost palpable despite the fact, as was told to me, that the Empress spent only about seven months in Cairo after the opening of the Omar Khayyam.

The Grand Stairway, wide and graceful and made of marble led into a large, beautiful, ornate room. A far cry from my little house in the woods that our neighbors built for us when ours burned soon after we moved to the country. To my surprise, I was not awed by all this grandeur. I felt very much at ease. I marveled at the changes God had brought about in my life. And here, in this place of splendor and pomp and history I thought of the ancient pharaohs. I imagined their goings and comings in their places of wealth and surplus and power. I later saw paintings on papyrus (a type of ancient paper) of Egyptians and their slaves. I met farmers carrying bundles of grain on their shoulders, and fishermen in their feluccas (fishing boats) trying to make a living from the Nile. There was the eight-year-old boy in a trade school for orphans. I bought a small rug he had made. It now hangs on the wall of my office in my house as a reminder, not so much of the City of Cairo, but of the people I met, of their dreams and their realities. Each time I look at it I thank God that He made us all in His image, and that His love reaches out to each of us. I also know that it is often *we* who make distinctions about where and how we live, but that He is Lord over all.

Twenty Feet of Snow and a Baptizing

I was in a small town above the Arctic Circle in Alaska. My mission was to be in charge of the music at a church where a Revival Meeting was to take place. This small church, with its congregation of about 40 people, was a mixture primarily of three groups of worshipers. There were the native Inupiat Eskimos, English speaking people, and Koreans. Cultures blended, yet each kept distinctive traits. This little (in numbers) church sponsored 5 mission outposts. The nearest was about 80 miles away.

During one of the weeks I was there a decision was

made that the visiting preacher and I should go to one of the Mission churches. It was about 135 miles away. In this land of ice and snow in the month of March, that was quite an undertaking.

There were only three available ways of travel: dog sled, snowmobile, or a small four-seater, one-engine airplane. One of the members of the home church volunteered to fly the plane. The forecast was for clear weather. The temperature was way below zero. However, before we could travel by air the plane had to be dug out of its snow cocoon. The engine had to be warmed overnight. The usual check system had to be carried out. The next morning we boarded the little plane. The pilot and preacher were in the cockpit area. I was in the seat behind the preacher. Survival gear took up all the remaining room.

As we moved down the short runway our pilot said, "Lola, you look to the left to see if anyone is coming." Turning to the preacher he gave similar instructions. "Look to the right. See if all is clear."

"All clear," we said, and we were on our route.

We followed a frozen river most of the time. Once we dropped low enough in altitude to visually track a moose into a thicket, then climbed a few hundred feet and were back on our way. We passed low over the small village of the 80-mile away Mission church and continued to our destination, fifty-five miles further. Our pilot called and gave our approximate arrival time. We soon began our descent.

There were no lights outlining a runway. There was no airport building. There was no airport! Then I saw it—the landing strip—a path carved out with a snowplow. Our experienced pilot set the plane down on the somewhat bumpy ice strip. He motioned for us to stay in the plane for a moment or two while he hitched it, much like hitching a horse, to a wooden pole frozen into the ground.

A person was waiting on a "snow-go" (short for snowmobile). Our pilot greeted the man, then turned to me. "Lola, you get on the snow-go and ride behind him to the church."

Who was I to question orders? I didn't know the man. He had no idea who I was, but he motioned for me to get on, and I did. The church was about the distance of two city blocks away. We took off. His driving was erratic, but I thought that maybe this was normal. I learned later that it wasn't. He had been drinking. To many inhabitants of the far North, alcohol is a scourge. He was, however, very kind and considerate.

He let me off at the door to the living quarters that were connected to the one room church. I knocked. The door opened. The man standing there said, "What are you doing here?"

I pointed to my two companions who were walking an icy path from the plane to the church. "I'm with them," I told him. "We came to worship with you today."

Soon afterward, our host, and a visiting preacher who was stationed there, began to make preparations for the service. Things were done in order. First, the church bell was rung to let the village people know there would be a worship service shortly. Second, two of the men checked the heating oil supply. Third, the man who greeted me at the door asked if I would play the small organ. It was not in mint condition, but that didn't really matter. The sweet voices of the women mingled with the deeper tones of the men as the first hymn of the service was sung, and there was praise in a way that surely must have pleased God.

Behind the pulpit I noticed a long narrow wooden box that looked much like a coffin. I wondered about it. There was a waterproof lining in it, and the outside was neatly covered with room paneling. After the service, I asked, "Has someone died?"

Our host looked at me thoughtfully and said, "Yes. Jesus

died, and was buried. Then He arose and walked this earth for a short time before returning to heaven. That's the reason for this box. In the cold months we cannot baptize in the river those who have claimed His salvation through His death, His burial, and His resurrection. So, we built this for that purpose."

"But you have no inside running water," I interjected. "How do you fill it?"

He laughed. "You city people!" he said, and grinned. "Sometimes I wonder if you could last two weeks here if you had to depend on your own working out of problems."

"Ah," I shot back at him. "Perhaps I'm not a city person. I'm not sure I'm a country person, either. I think I'm both."

"You can't be both," he said.

"Do you want me to prove it?" I asked.

"Sure." By now, we were playing a little cat and mouse game.

"Okay. Let me give you my solution to this problem. I've never used it for something like this, but I have used it."

"Let's hear it," he said. "Then we'll know."

"You have little water, but lots of snow and ice. Fill several buckets with snow and ice. Bring them in. Set them on the heater and the cook stove and let the cold stuff melt. You'll have water. Do that until you have enough to suffice in your baptistry."

He looked at me thoughtfully, then questioned, "How would you empty the baptistry?"

"The same way it was filled—by the bucketful."

"You're good," he said, "for a city girl." I was pleased that he could not, by looking and listening to me, know that living in the country was my life, but that my upbringing took place in the city, and that was part of my life, too.

I had still another question. "How do you perform the actual immersion in such a small, shallow pool?"

It was his time to answer. "This," and he gestured

toward the box, "will serve its purpose until someday we can do better. As for now, we have the person sit in the water. The pastor lowers his body the rest of the way as a symbol of the death and burial of Jesus, then lifts him to a standing position as the symbol of Christ's resurrection."

When All Is Said and Done

I awoke one morning, a bit perplexed about what to do. There were so many things that seemed important, and so little time in which to get them all done. My thoughts strayed to the days of meager fare after we moved from the city, and then to today. In spite of the disadvantages, those were busy times much as today. Money was a larger problem then than now, but today it still has to be earned.

Education is another medium in which progress was made over the years. Education and economics of that day and this would not even recognize each other.

Today, many country homes hold their own with, or are better than, those found in cities. Visiting in the city is no big deal. Traveling overseas isn't either. However, understanding cultures and habits and customs of peoples of other countries has not changed as much in many nations as in ours. I found myself thinking of these things and prayed, "Father, what am I supposed to do with what You've taught me?" The answer came clearly, " Follow Me, and you will need and use all that you have learned." There seemed to be an added emphasis. "You will put it ALL to use. You have special knowledge and insights that will be of value in your walk with Me."

Sometimes I am impatient for His next adventure. I find myself almost going ahead until I think of a long ago story of a sea captain and his chief engineer. They were arguing as to which of them was more important to the smooth sailing of the ship. Each thought he was needed most. They reached an agreement in order to find out. They would swap positions. A short time later the captain (acting as Chief Engineer) came rushing onto the deck, calling loudly to his new superior. "Chief," he yelled. "I can't make the ship go."

The "Chief" looked up sheepishly. "I've run her aground."

In His Word the Lord emphasizes, "Walk with Me" and "Follow Me". He is the true Chief of our universe. Sometimes we, by the way we live, appear to be trying to take over His job—the running of that universe.

He has work for us to do here. He orders our steps. He supplies our needs. When we try to take over His job, we run our lives aground.

PART FOUR

THE ANSWER

God has supplied my every need—from the time I was born until this present day. In the supplying, He has cared for me, been my teacher, my disciplinarian, my provider, my comforter. He has loved me and forgiven me in spite of the times I have disappointed, and yes, even betrayed Him. He has built for me a mansion. He has confirmed my belief in Him. Before me lies the greatest adventure I will ever know.

Why has He done this? I believe the answer lies in my willingness to follow Him wherever He would lead me. Life is not a bed of sweet roses, but rather a briar thicket full of thorns that often cause pain, but whether among the roses or the thorns God is there, and the sweet savor of His love permeates everything.

Those are the reasons I am where I am.